THE HOLY WELLS
OF
IRELAND

THE HOLY WELLS
OF
IRELAND

Patrick Logan

illustrated by Jim O'Callaghan

COLIN SMYTHE
Gerrards Cross 1980

First published in 1980 by Colin Smythe Limited,
P.O. Box 6, Gerrards Cross, Buckinghamshire

British Library Cataloguing in Publication Data

Logan, Patrick
The holy wells of Ireland.
1. Holy wells – Ireland
2. Christian shrines – Ireland
I. Title
263′.042′415   BX2320

ISBN 0-86140-026-7
ISBN 0-86140-046-1 Pbk

Printed in Great Britain
Typeset by Inforum Ltd, Portsmouth
Printed and bound
by Billing & Sons Limited
Guildford, London & Worcester

To
Michael J. Molloy
playwright, seanachie and
my friend

Contents

Illustrations

by Jim O'Callaghan

Preface

I should explain that this book was not planned: it happened. It began as an effort to investigate the healing which is believed to occur at holy wells and from this beginning it went on to study the ritual carried out around the wells and at other places of pilgrimage. This is an enormous subject, and soon I realised that there are some thousands of holy wells in Ireland, far too many to fit into a book of this size. It has therefore been necessary to make a selection and I have done this, realising that many interesting wells and pilgrimages have not been mentioned.

A study of the pilgrimages to Irish holy wells will reveal many examples of pre-Christian ritual and also the remarkable fact that these have survived in many cases until the present day.

I have not written this book to convince anybody of anything, but it would seem to me that something which has continued for more than fifteen hundred years is worth a little study. I would hope that, by reading it, some people might see their own background more clearly and understand a little of what their ancestors hoped and felt over the centuries. This would certainly please me, but I must admit that I have written this book to please myself.

My thanks are due to many people who generously gave me help. I would mention the late Eamonn de h-Oir and the staff of the Place Names Commission, who were all most helpful. I must also thank my friend Mr. Sean O'Nuallain of the Archaeological Section of the Ordnance Survey, and his assistant Mr. Patrick MacLoughlin, who have always made me welcome. My old friend, Michael J. Molloy of Miltown, Co. Galway, was kind enough to share some of his knowledge of holy wells and such things with me, and was always happy to find answers to my questions. Miss Christine Finnegan made the final corrections of the manuscript, no small undertaking, when I had been working on it. I must also mention and acknowledge gratefully the help given me by Miss Patricia O'Brien

11

and Miss Mona Watters. Much of the hard work was done by Miss Maire Gavan Duffy of the Swift Secretarial Bureau, who succeeded in reading my crabbed script and bringing it into order. I am very grateful to them all.

Patrick Logan,
Castleknock.

I

Introduction

To write a complete study of Holy Wells is almost impossible because the cult can still be found in many parts of the world and it is certainly older than recorded history. Probably it has survived better in Ireland than elsewhere in Western Europe but it still flourishes in the Middle East, in India and in many parts of Africa.

The reasons why it has survived so long in Ireland are complex. Our religious history since the Reformation and before it has been difficult and this appears to be important. It will be remembered also that many of the wells were famous for their power to heal diseases, powers which were attributed to the patron saint. As part of the cult there is usually a story to explain why the saint left the supernatural healing power in the well. It is remarkable that the cult still flourishes and shows many features and practices which are certainly pre-Christian, but now the entire ritual has been wrapped up in a cover of Christianity and at first look it appears to be Christian.

In a television interview some time ago Professor Pronsias MacCana, Professor of Old Irish in University College Dublin spoke of 'the extraordinary symbiosis' which has occurred in Ireland between Christianity and the Ancient Religion which it superseded. This symbiosis is very well seen in any study of Irish holy wells, and the more closely it is studied the more clearly it will appear that the cult began as primitive natural religion in which the well was often sacred.

As might be expected, many people dismiss it all as childish superstition and look forward to the time when man will have given up such childish things, but this is to misunderstand the spiritual and psychological needs of many people. The materialist cannot understand these needs and will therefore disapprove of the pilgrimages, but he is only the latest in a long line of self-assured people who for hundreds of years have condemned them and wished to have them discontinued.

Charles Plummer in his study of the *Lives of the Irish Saints* estimated that there were about 3,000 holy wells in Ireland. Certainly there are few parishes in which there is not at least one, but in many parishes there are more. Some wells may be found only after a search, because they have fallen out of favour and are being forgotten. In the area of County Dublin, Dr Kevin Danaher found ninety-nine holy wells and references to one hundred and eighteen are recorded in the Ordnance Survey Office. Even this figure may be too low.

It would be impossible in a book of this size to give even the name and position of every holy well in Ireland. Some of them are shown on the large scale Ordnance maps but most of them are not shown, or even mentioned in the *Ordnance Survey Letters*, written around 1838. In order to attempt a comprehensive list it would be necessary to visit every parish in Ireland and even then the list would not be complete: the sites of so many have been forgotten.

We are lucky that during the nineteenth century some men took care to examine the wells and wrote down what they heard or saw and from these records it is possible to learn about customs and rituals which were practiced before the Great Famine in the middle of the nineteenth century. Some of the writers, notably O'Donovan, O'Curry and their colleagues of the Ordnance Survey staff, wrote with understanding and a degree of sympathy, but many others, Page, Dixon-Hardy and Ousley, wrote with extreme dislike of what

Clocháns on Sceillig Mhichil. Little Sceillig is seen in the background. See p. 147.

they saw as 'superstition' and 'idolatry'. In their efforts, sincere according to their lights, they have recorded a number of valuable details which might not have been mentioned by more sympathetic witnesses. It will be noticed by anyone who reads these accounts, that the writers often say that some wells had ceased to be treated as holy and were no longer visited, but it will also be noticed that some new pilgrimages began and were popular during the nineteenth century. Some of these are still popular.

As it is impossible to mention all the pilgrimages, a selection must be made. No doubt some very interesting and popular wells will be omitted and for that I apologise in advance. My hope is to describe a number of the pilgrimages which seemed of interest to me and in addition to mention some other beliefs and practices which were to some extent related to them – cursing stones for example, or methods of keeping cattle healthy.

Writers during the nineteenth century did not often describe the pilgrimage in detail. Most of them just referred to the practice of walking barefoot, or on the hands and knees, around the well, or around a tree or a stone, and then went on to write about the drinking and fighting which were part of most Pattern Days. It is clear that the ritual was much the same at all the pilgrimages. Where older descriptions are available I have used them, but in general I have visited the holy well and learned the details of the pilgrimage. Nowadays the tendency is to shorten and simplify the ritual but in most cases details of the older practices are remembered.

This custom of visiting holy wells is mentioned in our oldest literature. There is the reference to the healing well which was prepared by the legendary physician of the Irish, Dian Cecht, and was used by him to treat the wounded at the Battle of Moytura. Christianized versions of the archaic stories about these wells can be found in the Lives of the Irish Saints, generally written before the thirteenth century. In some of these stories the saint was said to have used the water of an existing well to baptise his converts and left a blessing on the well. In other cases he caused the well to appear by working a miracle, or in some very special cases the saint was able to overcome and displace the druids who previously had been in charge of the well or he was able to drive a malevolent monster from the well where it had lived, so making it safe for his converts.

It is necessary to examine these old stories – even if it is not necessary to believe that they are all literally true – because in many cases echoes of the stories can be heard when people tell about their local holy wells and it will be realised that they express the opinions of the time they were written. In this way, beliefs and practices can be traced back for at least 1000 years – a number of them are mentioned by Geraldus Cambrensis in the twelfth century – and it is clear that many of them are derived from the primitive pre-Christian religion of the Celts. Here there is a danger of getting lost in a fog of myth and imagination so no theories will be offered to explain the practices. It will be enough to present the facts.

The most surprising thing about these practices is that they have survived to the present day. Ever since the Reformation they have been frowned upon by the English authorities, and by the Reformed Church. Later the civil authorities feared, or said they feared, what might follow such large and riotous assemblies as occurred at the better know patterns and in 1704 an Act of the Irish Parliament forbad the practice, with a penalty of a whipping or a fine of 10/-. Some ecclesiastics of the Established Church wrote against the pilgrimages as superstitious and idolatrous, and indeed a good case might be made for their opinions.

Some of the authorities of the Catholic Church also condemned the practices, mainly the drunkenness and faction fighting which often took place at the patterns. The police tried to stop what might be thought of as 'riotous assemblies' but despite everything the pilgrimages continued. Clearly they were able to provide something which people needed, and the popularity of the healing wells shows that many of the pilgrims derived benefit from the visit.

Psychologists will explain this benefit in their own terms, and all the better that they should do so, but they will agree that a pilgrim will be just as grateful to the saint as to the doctor for the relief of his headache, no matter what may have caused it. Even if today psychologists or psychiatrists claim to confer the same benefits in treating psychosomatic diseases, this was not well understood a hundred years ago by doctors or by patients. We now know that for nearly half of people's complaints no physical cause can be found, so on balance the advantage would be with the holy well rather than with the qualified doctor.

In some cases the pilgrims did not visit a holy well. The visit might be paid to a holy island or some other holy place. During the nineteenth century it was the custom to walk the station barefoot and some people still do this as at Lough Derg. This is not surprising because until recently many people in Ireland went barefoot during the summer months and a pair of boots was a status symbol. Part of the stations may have been done on the bare knees and this was mentioned by many writers, usually with horror at the sight of sore bleeding knees. Vigils and fasting were part of some pilgrimages:

they are part of the Loch Derg pilgrimage and of some other pilgrimages today. In practice the vigil sometimes became part of the festival and under normal conditions keeping vigil in June or July is no great hardship.

Some pilgrimages began during the nineteenth century, and the ritual at these modern pilgrimages is similar to that at the older ones. The pilgrims walk around the well, drink the water, go barefoot and collect the saint's clay, as though people insisted on following the ancient ritual.

The places associated with the saint, a holy island, an ancient monastic site, or an old burial ground, may be regarded as specially sacred. Clay from some of these places is used to prevent or cure diseases and in one famous case the clay from St. Mogue's Island was used to protect a house against fire. One story was of a pilot in the R.A.F. whose aircraft always came home safely during the war because there was some clay from St. Mogue's Island aboard it. In addition there was the promise of the saint that all those buried in this clay would be assured of heaven and to this a threat was sometimes added – if any of the saint's people dared to be buried elsewhere they would be condemned to hell. The origin of this legend was probably because the funeral offerings were paid to the clergy of the parish where the burial took place. There can be few Irish lakes which have not got a holy island and similarly many islands around the coast contain the remains of ancient monastic settlements. It is usually said that the missionaries of the early Irish church sought to settle in remote places but why did they settle on Scellig Mhichil, the most inaccessible rock on the Irish coast? Despite the grave inconvenience, people still continue to bury their dead on some of these islands and in some places it is a privilege carefully and jealously guarded by certain families. It would seem that many of these islands were holy places long before Christianity became the religion of the Irish.

Other things associated with these pilgrimages are stones and trees. The most usual trees are whitethorn, hazel and ash, and formerly oak, but holly, rowan and yew are also found near wells. In a few cases the 'well' is found in a hollow in the stump of a tree. There are, of course, stories of the origin of the tree which is often said to be immortal, and due to a miracle of the saint. Sometimes there is a sacred stone at or near the well and part of the pilgrimage may be a visit to and prayers at this special stone. The stone may bear the marks of the saint's feet, hands or knees, and there are often stories to explain why and how the imprints were made. In other cases the flat top of the stone may contain one or several small bowl-like hollows called *bullauns*, and the water which may be found in these is specially efficacious. Rounded stones which are often found in these *bullauns* may be used as curing stones or as swearing stones or as cursing stones. In some cases the special stone is a flat flagstone, which may be raised a little above the ground and some of the pilgrims may crawl under it. At some pilgrimages the holy stones may be arranged in the form of a 'chair', a 'bed' or a 'trough' where the pilgrims may sit or lie, whichever is the custom, in order to be cured of some ailment or by doing this he may be preserved from some danger. Often it will be found that a cross in one form or another has been cut on the stone, and at some pilgrimages the pilgrims each scratch a cross on the stone. The most mysterious of the stones are those in which holes have been made. They may be part of the station but nobody has given a satisfactory explanation of why the holes were made. Similar stones are found in Britain and as far east as India and it seems likely that they are older than Christianity.

The most dramatic stories are those which tell of stones which floated. Some of these stones are still to be seen and are provided with a story to explain why this power has been lost. The stories read like entries for a tall story competition, one outdoing the other until the winning story, told of a stone which brought Joseph of Arimathea, and a selection of other saints, from Palestine to Iona calling at Tara in Ireland and at the Isle of Skye in the Hebrides on the journey.

There are many other practices which must be mentioned. There are the methods of protecting the livestock against dangers, real or imaginary. There are the various methods of preventing or of curing mental illness, and methods of calming storms at sea. There were wells at which the future might be foretold and methods of preserving people from sudden death. There were wells which moved if insulted and ill luck was sure to follow the enemy who did wrong to the well or the tree or the stone.

These pilgrimages, and their associated practices, are not now so popular as they were a century ago, but it is of interest to notice that John O'Donovan, around the year 1840, often said that a certain pilgrimage had been discontinued, pilgrimages which today attract thousands of pilgrims. More often however he found that, while the faction fighting and drinking had ceased, people continued to visit the well on the prescribed day. This appears to have happened in the south-east of Ireland following the Wexford Rebellion in 1798. Since then some of these have regained their popularity, notably the pilgrimage to Lady's Island in Co. Wexford. It should also be said that the Catholic Church now encourages this visiting and praying at holy wells. Many of the praying areas have been tidied up and the pattern day may have been changed from 1st February, St. Brigid's Day, to a Sunday in summer when the weather is likely to be pleasant. All this has led, in some cases, to a revival of interest in the well.

The use of water for baptism and in other ceremonies of the Christian Church probably helped to Christianize this well worship and in the Gospels the Pool of Bethesda was mentioned as a healing well. There is also the reference to the Pool of Siloe where Jesus told a blind man to wash his eyes, and when the man did this his sight was restored to him. This dramatic story may account for some of the cures at the numerous eye wells which are found all over Ireland.

Looking forward to the end of this century it seems likely that the popularity of some of these pilgrimages will grow less. This might have been thought many times in the past when all the authorities agreed that the practice should stop, yet it has continued because it was something which people needed and enjoyed. Apart from the prayers and the ritual, the pattern was treated as a rural holiday and enjoyed as such. Pilgrims in any age are not notable for their piety, the Canterbury Tales make that clear, but anyone who has ever gone on a pilgrimage knows it is a memorable and enjoyable experience – something which is part of the nature of man. These days pilgrims may be called tourists.

II

The Pilgrimage

The exact ritual carried out by the pilgrims to the holy well is not often described in adequate detail and in order to learn about it, it is necessary to ask people who have been making the pilgrimage regularly for a number of years. In recent times, with the decline in popularity of many of the pilgrimages, the smaller details are being forgotten and very often the pilgrimage is carried out with little attention to them. During the last few years, the Church authorities have reorganised some of the pilgrimages and this has led to a revival of the popularity of the wells, especially in the cases in which the date was changed to a more suitable one. It is not possible to describe every pilgrimage, but it could be said that they are almost all variations on the same theme. Here a few pilgrimages will be described in detail, but some unusual points of the ritual may also be mentioned.

The routine at such notable pilgrimages as Loch Derg and Cruach Patrick are well known and have been described many times by witnesses, some of whom were friendly and some hostile. The practice at the great majority of pilgrimages was much less dramatic and the general picture may be like this. After some preliminary prayers – usually five decades of the Rosary – the pilgrim approaches the well and kneeling there says a few more prayers. Then he goes right-handwise round the well reciting more prayers. This circuit is made three times. Then he drinks some of the water and may dip his hand in it, and bless himself with the water. Often there is a special tree or a bush near the well on which he may hang a votive offering or he may leave one on the ground near the well. In some cases there is a carved stone at which the pilgrim may pray or around which he may walk. He may also pray at or walk round a tree and there may be a number of other stations at which the pilgrims pray. Another common practice is that the pilgrims each add a stone to a nearby heap. Some parts of the pilgrimage may include walking on the knees, or on the hands and knees, or walking through a stream. These practices of walking round trees, wells and stones, and walking on the knees, were most usually noted by hostile witnesses who were horrified by them and saw them, only, as primitive barbarism and superstition. Such opinions are those of the outsider, and the critics did not understand what the pilgrims thought about the practices: they would never ask. If they did ask they would learn that the pilgrims did not worship the tree, or the stone, or the well, they honoured them for their association with the saint; the stone might have been set up by him, and the well was often brought into existence by his supernatural power. Modern scholarship often disproves these beliefs, but the pilgrims knew nothing of this and still continue to honour their saint and the things associated with him in the traditional way.

In the parish of Outeragh in Co. Leitrim, the most usual day for making a pilgrimage is the 1st of February, the feast of St. Brigid, the patron saint of the parish. The rosary was recited by the pilgrims singly or in groups, as they walked towards the old graveyard and the writer can remember the murmur of the prayers heard in the darkness of the morning as the groups of pilgrims approached. The pilgrim entered the graveyard and first walked three times round an old ash tree, which stood near the site of the medieval parish church. Again, I remember being checked as I began to go round the tree to the left. A few Our Fathers and Hail Marys were said while going round the tree. The pilgrim then repeated the ritual at another tree and then returned to the site of the old church where he knelt near a carved stone which was said to represent the head of St. Brigid. Again a few Our Fathers and Hail Marys were repeated and it was the custom to leave a few pennies on the ground near the stone. When, a few years ago, the stone was examined and cleaned, it was found to be a corbel and the face could be seen to be bearded.

The pilgrim then went along a lane and across three fields to St. Brigid's well saying another rosary as he went. At the well, he knelt and prayed for a few moments before walking three times round the well. He then drank some of the water from the well and might leave a rag tied on one of the bushes near the well. Religious medals, fragments of rosaries, small crosses and other such things were thrown into the well or left on the ground around it. A third rosary was recited as the pilgrim returned home.

When O'Donovan visited the parish in 1836, he said that the saint's well was within a few yards of the old graveyard, and this is shown on the earliest Ordnance map. On a close examination of the site, I was unable to find any trace of the old well, but I did hear the story of how the well was closed up by an enemy and then miraculously appeared at its present site. There is another well about 250 yards away which may also have been a place of pilgrimage, because when cleaned out in about 1900, many religious objects were found in the mud taken from the bottom of the well. It may have been that when the original well was closed, this well was visited before the miraculous appearance of the present well.

Clonmacnoise was, and is, a notable place of pilgrimage. Formerly the pattern day was the 9th September, the feast of St. Ciaran, but now the day is the first Sunday of September. Pilgrims now do what is called 'the Short Station' and there was no rule about how this should be done; but some people still do 'the Long Station' and this was usually done by barefoot pilgrims. The Long Station begins at St. Ciaran's Well which is a few hundred yards from the ancient graveyard, and as the pilgrim comes to it, he kneels and says some prayers – usually a decade of the rosary. He then makes a circuit of the well and of the whitethorn tree beside it and may hang a votive offering on the tree or throw one into the holy well. The tree is a very special one: it has no thorns. It is commonly said that the water of the well cannot be boiled. By leaving the votive offering the pilgrim leaves his disease behind him.

From the well he moves on to a stone cross close by where he again kneels and says another decade of the rosary before going around the cross. He then moves on to a flat stone called 'the slab' where the ritual is repeated. There is still another stone to be visited, one on which a face has been carved. Here, in addition to the usual prayers etc., the pilgrim kisses the face. This circuit of well, cross, slab, and face, is carried out three times and each time the pilgrim crosses the little stream which flows from St. Ciaran's Well. This ends the first part of 'the Long Station'.

The pilgrim then moves on towards the High Cross in the graveyard and as he goes says five decades of the rosary. First he kneels at the High Cross and says the usual decade. Then round the cross and on to the little mound beside 'the Protestant Church', where the ritual is repeated. Next, he moves to St. Finian's Church, where it is again repeated and from there he moves around the perimeter of the graveyard, as always, in a clockwise direction, and back to the High Cross. This circuit is carried out three times and when he has completed the third circuit, he goes on his hands and knees from the High Cross to the site of the high altar in the ruined cathedral, where he says five Paters and the Creed.

The next circuit begins at the Little Cross with the usual prayers and circuit. From there he moves to the Cathedral and repeats the process. The other praying stations on this circuit are St. Ciaran's Little Church, 'Cartland's Church', 'Claffey's Church' and back to the Little Cross. This circuit is completed three times and at the end of it the pilgrim recites the complete rosary, fifteen decades.

Next, the pilgrim goes to the Nun's Church, where he again kneels and prays. There are three small mounds near this church and he goes round each of them three times. He then goes round the church three times and then goes inside and kneeling at the high altar says fifteen Paters.

He then goes to St. Finian's Well saying the rosary as he goes and kneeling at the well says fifteen Paters. It is not necessary to walk around this well: it may be covered by the water of the River Shannon or, in very dry weather, there may be no water in it. This is the end of the Long Station. My informant, Mr. Jack Claffey, a man aged about sixty, told me that he had done this pilgrimage every year for forty years, but added, rather apologetically, that the last time, he had not done it barefoot – his rheumatism was troubling him. I have calculated that it would take at least four hours to complete this routine.

Tobar na Mult (Well of the Wethers) also know as An Tubrid More, is at Ardfert, Co. Kerry. I have not visited this well, but the pilgrimage was described in detail in the *Kerry Archeological Journal* in 1911. The *turras* begins at 'the grave', where the pilgrim kneels and says five Paters and five Aves and then offers the round for the desired intention. He then walks around 'the grave' three times while saying five decades of the rosary, which was normally finished while the pilgrim again kneels at 'the grave'. He then begins a second rosary still at 'the grave' and completes it as he goes three times round the well. In all cases he must take care to move in a clockwise direction. He then goes to 'the Altar' where he kneels and completes a third rosary. Formerly it was the custom that the pilgrims now went into the well and dipped three times under the water. This total immersion is no longer practised but, instead, he takes three sips of the water and three times puts some of it on his face. He then returns to 'the altar' where he kisses each of the three figures on the altar stone. Alternatively, he may sign each of the figures and himself with the Sign of the Cross. This completes the pilgrimage.

Recently I paid a return visit to Lassair Well in Kilronan parish, Co. Roscommon. It is on the brink of Loch Mealey and near the ruins of the medieval parish church and a notice near the well gave details of how the traditional pilgrimage should be carried out. As the pilgrim approaches the well, he turns left towards a small grove where he kneels facing the well and says five Paters, five Aves and five Glorias. Next he returns to the well and again goes round it while saying two more decades of the rosary, and returns to the start where again the five Paters, Aves and Glorias are repeated. Then he goes back to and around the well while finishing the rosary. When all this is done, the pilgrim kneels at the entrance to the well but he does not go inside the surrounding wall. There he says ten Hail Marys in honour of St. Lassair, and asks the saint to place his petition in the hands of Our Lady. He then goes to a hollow stone which is on the right hand bank of the stream which flows from the well into the lake beside it. The oval hollow is about $18'' \times 12''$ and is known as the Holy Font of St. Ronan or the Cleansing Stone and he washes his feet, face and hands in the water in the Holy Font. Finally, he returns to the well where he kneels and says nine Hail Marys for his deceased friends. He then goes inside the wall to the well and finally ends by taking three sips of the water.

The notice does not mention votive offerings but on the wall around the well, I noticed a small pile of medals, crosses, rosary beads and statues, as well as a few rags tied on the bushes and a small box for offerings. Clearly, this is still a popular pilgrimage and the well and the area around it are neat and well maintained by a parish committee.

The symbolic purification by washing is the most interesting point of this pilgrimage. Similarly, at Tobar Muire near Elphin in Co. Roscommon, the pilgrim washes his hands and feet in the water of the stream which runs off from the well. Some people still do the pilgrimage to Tobar Muire barefoot, but this is not mentioned in the description of the pilgrimage to Kilronan.

It would be easy to describe the ritual of many other pilgrimages, but this would add little more to our knowledge of what people formerly did during their visits to holy wells. Some of the pilgrimages were described during the eighteenth and nineteenth century and these writers sometimes mention customs which now may be forgotten. It will be realised that the evidence of a hostile witness may be more valuable than that of a witness who favoured the practice of visiting the wells: the hostile witness is more likely to mention the more unusual features, which to him might seem superstitious or at least bucolic.

There is a famous pilgrimage to Malin Well near Malin Head, Co. Donegal, which was described by a writer in the *Donegal Annual* in 1970. In this case the well was a natural basin of fresh water formed in the rock and covered at high tide. It was blessed by St. Muirdhealach and had a 'cure'. This was a very famous well and the pilgrimage was described many times during the eighteenth and nineteenth centuries, almost always by hostile or unbelieving observers.

This is what Bishop Pococke wrote about it in 1752:

> Coming near the sea cliff I looked for the house I was going to, and could see none but came to a passage down the cliff where I found the house on the beach under the rocks, and enquiring for the well they showed me a hollow under a rock at the south end of a high small rocky island which at low water is a peninsula. Here people bathe with great success, the water being very salty as not mixed with fresh. And the Roman Catholics plunge in with superstitious notions that the water received some virtue from the saint (Muirdhealach) who lived in a cave in the rock of the cliff where poor people lodge who come for cure.

Mac Parlan, a hostile witness who wrote fifty years later, gave some more details:

> It probably, however, is near this old church, or the site of it that a famous pilgrimage is performed on some certain day in summer, at a creek of the sea which comes in among the rocks of Mawlinhead, by dropping a great number of beads: some walking on their legs, some on their knees, and some stationary, all vehemently whispering prayers: but the ceremony finishes something like the Indian Tamarodee, by a general ablution in the sea, male and female all frisking and playing in the water stark naked and washing off each other's sins.

At Mulhuddart in Co. Dublin, the holy well there dedicated to Our Lady, is still visited on the 8th of September and some other days and is said to cure sore eyes. At present the ritual is a very simple one: the pilgrim goes round the well three times before bathing his eyes with the water and drinking some of it. Luckily, there is a description of the well and the pilgrimage, written about 1744 by a hostile witness, Isaac Butler. He wrote:

> A small distance S'ward of the Chu' is a reputed Holy Well being much frequented on 8th Sept'r being Lady Day as people generally call it . . . This well is surrounded by a wall and some large trees, and about 5 years ago hath been vaulted over. On each end are two little uprights of stonework, like Chimnies in the front of each a small niche, one glazed (the other broken) and containing inside a cross from w'ch hangs a plate of brass and the Virgin Mary and Our Saviour lying in her lap after Crucifixion and distant view of Jerusalem relieved thereon – on each side a phial

bottle with artificial flowers and some mutilated little bodies representing I suppose the ascension of souls. All this work (to w'ch there is a great adoration) hath been done when the well was covered by some nunnery in Dublin. There's a hole in each end – the people lye on their bellies there with their head over the water repeat a prayer and drink and repeat another prayer before the little glazed bauble.

There have been some changes since 1744. The trees around the well are nearly all gone, and the water level is now lower than it was in the eighteenth century. I found it quite impossible to drink the water in the way Butler said it had been done, and I could not hear of any memory of this practice. The little house over the well is still exactly as described, with the holes in the ends where the pilgrims could drink the water. The well area is kept neat and tidy and the well house whitewashed by Mr. William Rae who lives close by. In 1975, a few days after the 8th of September, I visited this well. There were obvious signs that people had been visiting it during the previous few days; the grass around the well had been trodden down and there were footprints all over the place.

It is of interest to learn of this popular pilgrimage so near to Dublin during the first half of the eighteenth century. It appears that the community of nuns of Grace Dieu were those who had the neat little well-house built and that they were able to live in Dublin through what was, officially at least, the period of the Penal Laws. Their interest in the Lady Well may have been due to the fact that before the Reformation their house was at Luttrellstown, near Mulhuddart.

St. Mullins, Co. Carlow, has long been a place of pilgrimage and people still visit St. Moling's Well there. The well was visited on 17th June, the feast of St. Moling, but a more important day was 25th July, the feast of St. James: There was also a pattern held there on the Sunday before St. James' Day, called Sumalens Sunday. The ritual of the pilgrimage is now reduced to the recitation of the rosary, but there is a description of the older ritual written by Canon O'Hanlon. He wrote:

'They first make on their knees the rounds of certain places three times, and also drink of the well: they then wade barefoot through the stream, through the Theachra or Thurrus, a small lane through which flows a stream from the Holy Well, while praying all the time. This lane, in summer time, is full of thistles, briars and nettles, so much so, that several times a person making the pilgrimage is completely hidden by them, and the place is soft

Lady Well, Mulhuddart, Co. Dublin. See p. 26—7.

under foot, with numerous sharp stones in the way, none of which may be removed. Next they proceed to each of the ruined chapels (there are four) in succession, and recite certain prayers at each of these stations. They finish each round by praying at the old cross. They then enter the largest of the ruined churches where they pray round an old stone slab there, nine times, saying a Pater and Ave each time, and placing a small stone on the slab after each round: then they go into the inner building and after praying under the east window where the altar once stood, they finish by putting a leaf in the window and kissing the stone under the window inside. They then come out and sitting down on a grave, put their shoes on their feet. They conclude by bestowing an alms on the poor, of whom there are sure to be several present on the feastdays referred to.'

This was certainly not an easy pilgrimage and O'Hanlon referred to the thorns which often had to be removed from the pilgrims' feet when they had finished. I learned in 1975 that the practice of walking in the stream is no longer carried out.

Formerly there was a popular pilgrimage to All Saints near Banaher, Co. Offaly. When O'Donovan visited All Saints Well (Tobar na Naoimh) in Reynagh parish, he also mentioned Lady's Well, and four other small wells, one of which was then dry. There was a pattern held at All Saints on the 29th of June, the feast of Sts. Peter and Paul, and on the Sunday before the 1st of August, but O'Donovan reported that they had been discontinued three years before his visit. At present the pilgrimage may be made at any time between 15th August and 1st November and when seeking a cure or making any other special request, people did it three times. As one approaches the old graveyard across a field path from the road the holy wells, said to be seven in number, were on the right hand side in a bank overlooking an area of bogland. The bog has been drained, and, in consequence, all the wells are now dry, but the grove of small whitethorns which grew near them is still there. The pilgrim knelt and prayed at each well, one after another, as well as making a circuit of each one, until he came to the seventh well which was nearest the entrance to the graveyard and was the most important one. There, he carried out the usual ritual, hung a votive offering on one of the whitethorns, drank some of the water and usually took some of it away.

The pilgrim then entered the graveyard and went to a heap of stones called 'the altar', where he might leave a medal, a coin, or some other offering. Offerings were also left at a modern statue of Our Lady. During a visit to All Saints in 1974, I failed to find either 'the altar' or the statue of Our Lady.

Many cures were claimed by pilgrims to All Saints. I was told that one of the wells cured sore eyes, another cured sores on the skin, another cured diseases of the head, etc., and a number of people mentioned what must have been a notable cure – a man with webbed toes. It was firmly believed that if a pilgrim seeking a cure were to hang a piece of cloth on the whitethorn and complete the pilgrimage, his disease would die away as the cloth rotted. In the days of its popularity, many pilgrims went to All Saints barefoot, but at present not so many go there.

During the past ten years or so, a number of pilgrimages have been revived and reorganised and the number of pilgrims has now increased. One of these was the pilgrimage to St. Brigid's Well in Cullienmore townland, Walshestown parish, Co. Westmeath, which formerly was visited on 1st February. Some years ago, Father Andrew Shaw, a curate in the parish of Mullingar, caused some

Jo'C '79

St. Brigid's Well, near Mullingar, Co. Westmeath.

alterations to be made in the layout of the area around the well and at the same time the special pilgrimage day was changed to the last Sunday in August.

The well area measures about 90 feet × 60 feet, with the longer sides facing east and west. The well itself, in about the middle of the south side, is covered by a half dome of stones and earth. At the north side of the area, a replica of an ancient Irish church has been built. The south wall of this building is absent and a stone altar is found in the opening, where Mass may be said in sight of the pilgrims. A short and well kept path leads from the road to the south east corner of the well area and, as he reaches it, a visitor will notice a flagstone on which is the word 'Welcome'. The praying stations are marked, each by a flagstone, fourteen of them, representing the fourteen Stations of the Cross, and the pilgrims move along a flagged circular path, pausing at each station. The first nine flagstones are on the pilgrim's left hand as he goes, and the final five are on his right hand and these are visited on a second circuit. At the end he drinks of the well water and as he leaves he will notice another flagstone which says, 'God be with you'. The stream from the well flows down through the centre of the area where it joins a stream from the fish farm a few yards away.

I visited St. Brigid's Well on the 25th August, the Station Sunday, in 1974. It was a pleasant afternoon and I counted about fifty cars along the narrow road. There were about five hundred people present, as many men as women, and of all ages, down to babies in prams. Many people took home bottles of the water, and I noticed one enthusiastic man who filled three large lemonade bottles at the well. Generally, it was a family outing, children with sweets and toys, and people appeared to be enjoying the pilgrimage.

I have been able to discover other pilgrimages at which there were fourteen praying stations. One was mentioned by Henry Morris who described many of the holy wells in Co. Donegal. He wrote:

'There is a peculiar *turas* at a place called Greenhills, near Ballylar National School where fourteen stones each marked with a cross are arranged in horseshoe shape.'

There were also fourteen praying stations on Inishark a holy island off the coast of Co. Galway.

Another pilgrimage which has recently been reorganised is that to Tobar Bhride at Brideswell in Co. Roscommon. I visited the well on a cold day in February 1976 and learned that some years ago the parish priest had reorganised it and said Mass at a portable altar placed near the well at midday on the pilgrimage day, the last Sunday of July. Two years ago, the bishop of the diocese said the Mass. In addition, the priest comes at 4.00 p.m. and conducts the station ritual.

The well and the praying stations are on what is called Brideswell Common, where a handball alley and the local primary school have been built. The well is deep and dark, rising from a limestone outcrop and surrounded by a wall, with a gate and steps leading down to the water. The strong stream from the well flows through a stone lined channel in the floor of what is called the water house. This is a square stone building, built of large blocks of the local limestone and at present one story high. It is about 20 feet square and the stream enters through an arch in the west wall and runs out through another arch in the east wall from where it flows to a *turlough* (winter flooded land) some distance away. The house is entered through a doorway in the north wall. The interior is like the old-fashioned cow byre with the 'group' to gather the manure in the centre. On the outside of the west wall over the well, there is an interesting slab of limestone bearing the arms of Randall Mac Donnell, first Earl of Antrim. The slab says that the water house was built by Mac Donnell in 1625 in gratitude to the saint.

The pilgrims begin just past the ball alley at a ring of stones, around which pilgrims walk saying five Our Fathers and five Hail Marys. This is repeated at a single ash tree on a small mound, and then the pilgrim goes to a large stone in the centre of the common. From the stone the pilgrims walk through the school yard through two gates which are always kept open. This journey from the stone to a modern statue of St. Brigid was formerly made on the bare knees. The pilgrim then prays and walks round the statue. He then enters the water house where he kneels on a rocky outcrop in the floor and ends the pilgrimage by saying the rosary and drinking some of the water. I did not hear anything about the sacred fish which lived in the well, or of any practice of bathing in the stream, but people around Bridewell are very proud of their pilgrimage, and one man told me that the next pilgrimage day is the 25th of July.

Another Co. Roscommon pilgrimage which has been successfully revived is made to Tobar Ogulla near Tulsk. It is said locally that the well is that one at which St. Patrick baptized the daughter of the king of Ireland, and formerly it was visited on St. Patrick's Day. The well is on the side of a large brook which in wet weather overflows into the well. On the opposite side of the brook from the well a platform had been built where Mass is said on the last Sunday of June. This revival has been encouraged by the Church and the bishop of the diocese of Elphin, himself a native of the district, has said the Mass on the station day, and people describe a miraculous cure which followed a visit to Tober Ogulla. The individual concerned, Mr. Jack Fox, believed to be suffering from malignant disease with jaundice, is still alive and now well.

The pilgrimage to the site of an ancient monastic settlement at Kilabuonia in the Barony of Iveragh, Co. Kerry, has some unusual features. There is a large cairn of pebbles left over the centuries by thousands of pilgrims, beside St. Buonia's Well which is near the south west corner of the monastic enclosure, and may be visited on any Friday, Saturday or Sunday. Nine rounds of the well are made and at the end of each round the pilgrims go to 'the priest's grave', where the rosary is said before doing the next circuit of the well. 'The priest's grave' is on an upper level of the enclosure near the ruined oratory and is covered by two sloping flagstones, one on the north side and the other on the south side. The triangular shaped ends are closed by two more flagstones, one on the east and the other on the west end. The flagstone which closes the west end has a circular hole 5″ in diameter cut through it just above the present ground level. The usual type of votive offerings, hairpins, buttons, shawl tassels, etc., are passed through this hole. North of 'the grave', there is a standing stone. It is part of the pilgrimage to scratch a cross on this stone with a pebble, and as a result, the crossed lines are now cut deeply.

Pilgrim praying in the well house at St. Brigid's Well, Liscannor, Co. Clare.
Notice the pictures and statues left as votive offerings. See p. 34.

Inside the grounds of Warrenstown College, Co. Meath, is a holy
well dedicated to St. John the Baptist. This well had been neglected
until 1944, when the Salesians, who run the college, had it tidied up.
The water now issues from a pipe and forms a small stream, When
the scrub around the well was being cleared, they found the remains
of a number of houses near the well.

Since the well area was improved, the number of pilgrims has
notably increased. The well is visited between the 23rd of June, St.
John's Eve, and the 29th of June, the feast of SS. Peter and Paul.
Here, the story is that the water was used by St. Patrick to baptise his

converts. It is especially popular on the night of 23rd – 24th of June, because is is believed that at midnight the water boils up and then for an hour afterwards the power of the water is greatest. I visited the well in September 1973, and noticed many pieces of cloth tied on a whitethorn near the well.

The most distinguished and best recorded holy well in Co. Clare is St. Brigid's Well at Liscannor. The well area is surrounded by an iron rail and pilgrims approach through a gate. As they enter, they kneel at a modern statue of St. Brigid and say five Paters, five Aves and five Glorias. They then move around the statue saying whichever prayers they wish. The pilgrims then climb some steps to the higher level and repeat the five Paters, Aves and Glorias as before. The third praying place is an old stone cross up a slight incline from the wall and here the prayers are repeated and the cross circled as usual. The pilgrims then go back down to the well which is on the lowest level. It is covered by a small house which contains a most elaborate collection of votive offerings, large pictures, statues, crutches, etc., etc. Pilgrims drink the water in the Name of The Father and of The Son and of The Holy Ghost, and their requests 'are immediately granted'.

This again is a pilgrimage which has been modernized and reorganised most efficiently and appears to be as popular as ever. At present the largest crowds visit the well on the 15th of August, but formerly it was visited on the evening before the first Sunday in August, and people spent the night by the well and carrying out the pilgrimage ritual.

III

The Holy Day

Among the prechristian Celts, the year was divided into four quarters. The beginning of Spring, February 1, was marked by the feast of Imbolc. Summer began with Beltaine, 1st of May, Autumn with Lughnasa, 1st of August, and winter with Samhain, 1st of November. There were other festival times and days but these, marking as they did the course of the seasons, were the most important. Some prechristian practices associated with these festivals were continued when Christianity had become the religion of the Irish and some of them are still seen after fifteen hundred years.

When detailed records of these practices were written down during the eighteenth century, it was clear thay they had been long established, though they are rarely mentioned in the native Irish records. Like many other things, they were taken for granted and it was only when strangers came and observed them that detailed descriptions were written down. There are, of course, some early references to them. The Loch Derg pilgrimage is mentioned in the 12th century and a number of times during later centuries. The pilgrimage to St. Mullins is mentioned in the year 1347 when Clyn said that the pilgrims walked in the water there. These were very famous pilgrimages and it would not be expected that the celebration of the parish holy day would be thought of as so important as to be written about. We know little about what the pilgrims did at these holy wells, and trees, and stones, before the destruction of the native civilization early in the seventeenth century. By the middle of the eighteenth century it was clear the holy wells were visited in every part of the country where the old religion had remained strong, and even in those parts of Ulster where the native race had been to some extent replaced by the new English and Scots, the practice continued.

Each parish had its pattern day. This was usually the feast day of the patron saint of the parish and was regarded as a holy day of obligation to hear Mass. This practice continued into the present century and even now in Seir Ciaran parish in the Diocese of Ossory, people do not work on the 6th of March, the feast day of St. Ciaran.

There are many stories about the evil which befell those who worked on the saint's day. One from the parish of Colmanswell, Co. Limerick, tells of a man who worked on the Saint's Day to earn some money, and as he passed by the holy well later, the ill-gotten money disappeared from his pocket. In Co. Leitrim, I heard of a stone mason who was so foolhardy as to work at his trade on St. Brigid's Day. People made all sorts of direful prophesies about what might happen and nobody was very surprised when the unfortunate man was blinded by a stone splinter.

There might be more than one holy well in the parish, and more than one pattern day, but the feast of the parish patron was the great day and a major holiday which sometimes continued for a few extra days. When the holy day fell during the summer, it would be expected that large crowds would attend, and in some cases as many as five thousand people are mentioned. At Clonmacnoise on the 9th of September, three to four thousand people attended and the pilgrims stayed for two days.

When the 'rounds' had been completed, people hurried to join the crowd and the pattern resembled any rural gathering such as a hurling match, a parish sports day, or a point-to-point race meeting. There was plenty of eating and drinking, courting and fighting, and all this was observed and described at length, mainly by outsiders. Here is a description of the crowd that gathered at St. Bartholomew's Well near Cork city on the 24th of August in 1778.

> We went this morning to that (well) of St. Bartholomew which being that saint's day was surrounded by vast crowds of Roman Catholics some upon their knees, at their devotion and others walking with their beads in their hands. This ceremony is here called a 'Patron'. The well is enclosed with trees close to the side of the road and even the sight of it looks refreshing. When their devotions were over they retired to several sutlers' tents erected for that purpose, some to eat and drink, others to wrestling and yelling, dancing, noise and merriment which brought on several boxing bouts while we stood there. In short it is exactly what we call a 'wake' in England setting aside the devotion.

These patterns occurred more usually during the summer and autumn, but many occurred at what would be thought unsuitable times. Spring still begins in Ireland on the first of February, the prechristian festival of Imbolc, but now this day is the feast of St. Brigid, one of the major feast days in the calendar of Irish saints. Wells and churches dedicated to St. Brigid are found all over Ireland and many of the pilgrimages to one of her wells are famous. Whatever the scholars may say about Brigid – whether there was one or many Brigids, or if she was a pagan goddess or a christian saint, or an amalgam of both – the essential point is that to the Irish she is still a great figure and almost the equal of St. Patrick.

One of her most famous wells is at Faughart, north of Dundalk in Co. Louth. At Faughart, there are many stories about the saint, such as the belief that she was a native of the district, built the local church, and plucked out her eyes in an effort to rid herself of an unwanted suitor. Other wells dedicated to St. Brigid in Co. Louth are those at Dunleer and in the parish of Marlerstown, and they are all visited on the first day of spring. Another centre of the cult of St. Brigid is at Kildare, where she is one of the patrons of the diocese and her well at Tully is visited by many people. Another is St. Brigid's Well at Cliffony in Co. Sligo, where a pattern was held on the first of February. The cult of St. Brigid was long established in the twelfth century when it was mentioned by Geraldus Cambrensis.

It would appear that this cult, for one reason or another, has become more widespread over the centuries. Brigid appears to have taken over the parish of Ardagh in Co. Longford, from St. Mel (6th February); her feast alone is now remembered there. Early in the 17th Century, Colgan wrote that the parish church of Killore, Co. Westmeath, was dedicated to St. Aodh, but he is no longer remembered there, and in O'Donovan's time, (1840), the pilgrims went to Tobar Brighde, near a small ancient church called Temple Brighide. The original patron saint of Outeragh Parish in Co. Leitrim, was Finnabhar, but he has been displaced by St. Brigid, and is completely forgotten there. There are some famous wells dedicated to St. Brigid in Co. Cork. One of these is at Castlemagner and its reputation for sanctity and for healing was such that large crowds used to visit it on St. Brigid's Day. Another well was in Buttevant Parish in a townland called Mountbrigid, and was even more famous.

In addition to St. Brigid, there is a group of well known saints whose feast days fall around the same time, and may also be survivals of the festival of Imbolc. Among these is St. Mogue, whose day was the last day of winter – 31st of January. He is honoured in many parts of the diocese of Kilmore, notably in Drumlane and Templeport parishes in Co. Cavan and at Rosinver in Co. Leitrim, where patterns were held on his feast day. He is also honoured in Ferns diocese, of which he is the principal patron and where his holy well is still honoured. He has another holy well in Clonmore parish, Co. Carlow.

St. Féchin's Day falls on the 29th of January, and he is honoured in many parts of Ireland. These extend from Termon Féchin on the east coast in Co. Louth, right across the country to Cong in Co. Mayo and to Omey Island off the coast of Co. Galway. Féchin is well remembered at Termon Féchin where many legends are told about his building the church there, but he is best remembered at Fore in Co. Westmeath, where the ruins of his very ancient church still stand near his well.

Two more of these festivals may be mentioned. In Kilaha parish, Co. Kerry, O'Donovan found that the 5th of February was kept as a holy day, but the name of no saint was associated with it. St. Fursa's Day fell on the 8th of February and is celebrated at Ullard near Graguenamanagh, Co. Kilkenny, where the holy well is credited with extraordinary powers – as well as curing diseases, it preserves people from shipwreck. The power of the water is increased if, before use, it is put in the hollows made by the knees of the saint in a stone found near the holy well.

The next important feast day is the 17th of March – St. Patrick's Day. This is, of course, the greatest day in the Irish Calendar and may be the day on which he died, because it marks no point in the calendar. The popularity of this day may also have been due to the fact that it was a break in the rigorous lenten fast. Wells, churches and parishes are dedicated to Patrick in many parts of the country and legends about his miracles and successes are heard everywhere. He may be said to have displaced the druids who were in charge of the well, or he may have used the water to baptise his converts, or the well may have sprung up in answer to his command.

A feature of these wells, is often a stone which bears the imprint of St. Patrick's knees, hands, feet, head, or in one case, on a stone at the old church of Cross Patrick in Killaha parish, Co. Mayo, the saint left the imprint of his bottom. Not far away from Cross Patrick, another stone bears the imprint of the knees of St. Patrick's ass. Once, I was foolish enough to ask a local man if he was sure that St. Patrick had visited the holy well in Carna townland at Mullaghhorne, Co. Cavan. He answered:

'Of course I am sure he came here. How else could he have left the track of his knees in that stone?'

This answer, I believe, explains why there are so many of these stones; they were thought of as the saint's visiting cards.

The cult of St. Patrick was not so popular in some of the southern counties. His wells are seldom found in Waterford, Cork or Kerry and people will tell you that he did not visit Co. Clare. As around St. Brigid's Day, there are some feast days of lesser figures around St. Patrick's Day. These included the feast of St. Ciaran of Seir Ciarain, on the 5th of March. O'Donovan mentioned a holy well called Tobar Fionain on Valencia Island, Co. Kerry, which was visited on the 17th of March by pilgrims who wished 'to keep sickness away from themselves.' In Glenbehy parish, the patron is St. Gregory, whose feast day falls five days before St. Patrick's Day. Still in Co. Kerry, in Dromod parish, there is a lake called Loch Luigheach, in which an island called Inis Uasal is holy. A pattern was held at this island on the 18th of March, St. Finan's Day. St. Finan was believed to have suffered from leprosy and to have cured lepers.

St. Senan's Day, the 8th of March, is honoured in North Kerry and in West Clare. St. Lachtainn is honoured in Co. Clare in Kilcorney parish and also in Kilnamona parish where Tobar Lachtin is visited on the 19th March. This saint is also honoured at Freshford, Co. Kilkenny, on the same day. O'Donovan also mentioned Kennanach's ancient church and holy well on Oilean dá Chruinne in West Galway, which was visited on the 12th of March.

Some holy wells are visited on Good Friday and others on Easter Sunday. It would seem that these pilgrimages are Christian in origin, but even here one might remember the custom of eating Easter eggs. O'Donovan mentioned a pilgrimage to a well called Tobar Naoimhéid in Kilscorbe parish, Co. Galway, which was held on Good Friday, but he also said that the well had gone dry. In Toomower parish, Co. Sligo, which was dedicated to St. Columcille, there was a pilgrimage on Easter Sunday. This was held, not at the site of an old church, but at what was called Kingstone Well (Tobar Cloiche Righ) in Greenan townland, and in Mullery parish in Co. Louth, Sunday's Well (Tobar Domhnaigh) is visited on Easter Sunday.

Some pilgrimages were made on Trinity Sunday, another major Christian feast. Perhaps the most distinguished of these is that made to Trinity Well, which is the source of the River Boyne. In Co. Louth, in Kildemock parish, Trinity Well is found on Trinity Green and is also visited on Trinity Sunday. In Termonfechin parish, Co. Louth, Trinity Well is visited on, as usual, Trinity Sunday. Another one was found, within the walls of Knocktopher Abbey House, Knocktopher, Co. Kilkenny and was described in 1873.

The next popular day for pilgrimages was May Eve or May Day, which marked the beginning of summer. There are many beliefs and customs associated with the first of May, and the decorating of the May bush is described elsewhere in this book. Many of the customs appear to be designed to protect the cattle and the growing crops. There were two Donegal wells which were visited on May Eve. These were Malin Well near Malin Head, and Tobar na n-Aingeal in Benndubh townland in Cill Aobhóg parish. Both these wells have been described many times. Tobar na n-Aingeal had a reputation as a healing well and it was believed that this power was much greater on May Eve.

In Co. Dublin there was a holy well at Diswellstown which was visited on May Eve. This was especially popular with those who suffered from sore eyes. At the well, it was the custom to light a candle and care must be taken to see that the candle is not extinguished. It was also the custom to bathe the sore eyes with a cloth which was then hung on a bush beside the well.

Some other wells which were, or still are, visited on May Eve may be mentioned. One of these is the seashore well at White Head, Co. Antrim. Another was Tobar an Ailt, near Loch Gill in Co. Sligo. This is still a popular well and some unusual powers have been attributed to its water, such as the power to increase the skill of football players.

Another popular day is the 9th of June, the feast of St. Columcille. Naturally, this man is honoured most in his native Donegal, but wells and churches dedicated to him can be found as far south as Ard Colum parish in Co. Wexford, where his well is visited on the 9th of June. In Co. Donegal, many of his holy wells are still popular. The most notable one appears to be in Glencolumcille, where Morris said that the *turras* was three miles long and a very arduous one. Recently R.T.E. news showed the Parish Priest, Father Mac Dyer, leading the pilgrims as they made the pilgrimage barefoot. Another is on the shore of Loch Columcille, and the lack of fish in the lake is said to be due to the left handed blessing given it by the saint. At Gartan, where Columcille was born, there is another of his wells. Also at Gartan, people visit what is believed to be his birth stone. A visit to this stone is said to cure loneliness.

Outside County Donegal, Columcille is popular in Mayo and in Galway. Two of his wells are described in Kilconickery parish in Galway, and near one of them there is a stone which bears the imprint of his knees. One of his wells has also been described on Iniskea North, a small island off the coast of the Mullet peninsula, which was the site of an ancient Irish monastic settlement. A more accessible well is in Oughval parish, also in Co. Mayo, beside an ancient ruined church. This was a famous well, which contained a sacred fish and had a cursing stone called St. Columcille's *leac*, near the well. This stone had been removed when O'Donovan visited the parish.

At Sandyford, Co. Carlow, O'Toole described St. Columcille's Well. This was said to be due to a miracle of the saint, who used the water to cure a man with disease of the head and face, and the water is still used to cure diseases. Both this well, and St. Columcille's Well in Durrow parish, Co. Westmeath, were able to defend themselves against their enemies.

The 24th of June, the feast of St. John the Baptist, was a popular feast day. In this case, as in some other cases, the ritual began at sunset on the previous evening, when fires were lit on hill tops to celebrate Bonfire Night. It seems certain that this festival began as a prechristian celebration of the summer solstice and the Beltanny tree, i.e., the May bush, was burned in the fire. Wells dedicated to St. John the Baptist are found in all parts of Ireland, and pilgrims gathered at them during the previous evening. It was the custom to wait by the well until midnight when it was believed that the water boiled up, and then for a further hour, 'the water could cure anything.'

Not all these midsummer wells are dedicated to St. John the Baptist. Near Downpatrick, in Co. Down, the Struel Wells, are visited at this time, and are dedicated to St. Patrick. Pilgrims first go to Mass in Downpatrick and take some clay from his grave there before going to Struel. There, according to Philip Dixon Hardy, some climbed the hill on their knees, while others each added a stone to a heap there. The water is channelled through different 'wells,' one of which is used to treat sore eyes, and another is called 'the Drinking Well.' At midnight, between the 23rd and 24th of June, the water rises and overflows in the large well and, as usual, its power is greatest at this time. Hardy also says that those who have not been cured by the newly risen water cry out eagerly 'Who has got the blessing?'

Another famous midsummer pilgrimage is to an island in Gougan Lake, seven miles from Inchigeela, and the source of the River Lee on the Cork – Kerry border. Pilgrims gather at the lake on the previous evening and cattle are driven through the water to preserve them from murrain. In the centre of the island, which is joined to the mainland by a causeway, Hardy mentioned a wooden pole which he believed was the remains of a large cross. He said that the pole was covered with votive rags and bandages, and the spancels of the cattle were also hung on the pole. A part of the lake adjoining the causeway was enclosed and covered in, and treated as a holy well, and Hardy described the pilgrims pushing and scrambling to get in to bathe in the 'well.' He also mentioned 'a piece of rusty iron' which was passed from one pilgrim to the next. He shows a sketch of a pilgrim with this 'piece of rusty iron' on his head. I could not decide what it may have been, but it was probably a relic of the local St. Barry and it was used to bless the pilgrims, just as the saint's bell was used at Cruach Patrick.

Morris described the ritual at a well called Tobar na mBan Naomh (Well of the Holy Women) near Teelin in Co. Donegal. Pilgrims went to the well on Midsummer Night and remained there all night if the weather was fine. The names given to the women were Ciall (Sense), Tuigse (Understanding) and Naire (Modesty) and it is believed that they grew up beside the well, became nuns, and blessed the well. Fishermen, when sailing out of Teelin Bay lower their sails in salute as they pass near Tobar na mBan Naomh. They also take off their caps, and ask the help and blessing of the three holy women as they pass near the well.

This is certainly a prechristian practice with a thin veneer of Christianity over it. It is also an example of the trios of saints or of goddesses which are often mentioned in connection with holy wells, and are a feature of ancient Celtic religion. Dillon mentioned the earth goddess as a source of fertility, who was worshipped in triple form as the *matres* (mothers). I have heard a legend about three nuns, accompanied by a big spotted cow, 'like an Ayreshire,' who were seen going from St. Brigid's Well at Ardagh, Co. Longford, towards Slieve Golry. In Irish mythology, we hear of three Brigids who were patrons of poets and of smiths.

O'Donovan described a midsummer day pilgrimage to St. Damhnat's Well in Lavey parish, Co. Cavan. The well, a cataract on a small stream, is called Eas Damhnait, and near it was a flagstone containing a large hollow. This hollow contained two or three quarts of water which was used by the pilgrims to bathe their sore knees. Cures were expected in this case because the hollow had been worn by St. Damhnat's knees.

A typical midsummer pilgrimage was to St. Laichteen's Well, six miles north west of Blarney in Co. Cork. This is still a popular pilgrimage and the well is visited on St. John's Day and also on the Sunday following. The well is also visited on June 26, St. Laichteen's Day.

Naturally, July is the great month for pilgrimages, because the weather is good and the days long. A popular day was the 25th of July, the feast of St. James, whose wells are found in Wexford, Limerick and Kilkenny and other areas which came under the influence of the early Normans. Less likely places are Kilgefin parish, Co. Roscommon, and Carraic a'Teampuill in Co. Sligo. It will be remembered that the great prechristian festival of Lughnasa to mark the end of summer, continued as a partly christianized feast on the last Sunday of July or the first Sunday of August. This festival has been examined very thoroughly by Maire Mac Neill, who showed that most of the Christian feasts between St. Mary Magdalen's Day, the 22nd of July, and the 15th of August, the Feast of the Assumption, were Christian efforts to replace the Lughnasa festival.

The pilgrimage to Tobar an Ailt, about three miles from Sligo town, is still very popular. It is beautifully situated in a natural grove and the trees, in full leaf on the pattern day, give a soft dim light like the inside of an old church, where people prayed silently or spoke softly. The well of lovely cold, clear water bubbles up at the foot of a steep, rock face and flows off towards Loch Gill a short distance away. I noticed that there were many hazel trees growing close to the stream and the nuts from the trees could fall into the water. A little way up the steep, rock face, a modern altar has been built where Mass was said twice on the pattern day – the last Sunday of

Tobar an Ailt near Sligo town.

July this year (1978). The praying stations around the well, fourteen of them, are referred to as 'altars' and certainly some of them resemble the 'praying altars' on Inishmurray. Each 'altar' – some of them are no more than small heaps of stones – is marked with a small modern cross made of marble numbered I to XIV, as on the Stations of the Cross in a Catholic church.

When I visited the well during the week before the pattern, I saw a number of people moving from one of the praying stations to the next, but on the pattern day very large crowds made the pilgrimage from early morning when Mass was said at 6.00 a.m. for those who may have spent the night at the well. When I got to the well for a Mass at midday, many hundreds of people were assembled and while I watched, five buses arrived with more pilgrims and as I left people were still arriving in large numbers. There was one stall which sold sweets, soft drinks and such things, but nobody was selling or buying anything else.

The well is in a valley which runs down to Loch Gill and just off shore there is an island called Inishmore which contains the ruins of an ancient church. A little way along the shore is Toberconnell Bay and an island dedicated to St. Connell. The name of the townland, Clochermore, would indicate the presence of a church, and it also contains an old graveyard, which may be where the church was.

At Tobar an Ailt, the pilgrimage has been completely taken over by the church and efficiently organized. Despite this, it still has the air of a country festival, where people meet their neighbours and exchange news and gossip, as they sit around and talk. The praying area is entered through narrow ways between boulders, which suggested to one pilgrim that he was going into a prechristian Celtic sacred grove. As I moved around under the trees, I wondered why Yeats, who knew the neighbourhood well – Dooney Rock and the Lake Isle of Inisfree are close by – never mentioned Tobar an Ailt in spite of his interest in strange religions and mysticism. At the time he was growing up in Sligo, Tobar an Ailt was not respectable.

In many cases, the old festival of Lughnasa is celebrated by visiting a well dedicated to a Christian saint and some of these pilgrimages were famous. One of these was at Mám Ean at the top of a mountain pass in west Galway. This well, which was dedicated to St. Patrick, was a great meeting place for people from both sides of the mountain on the last Sunday of July. There are many legends about this meeting and it had been identified as a Lughnasa feast by Mac Neill.

Another one is the pilgrimage to St. Ciaran's Well at Castle-keeran near Kells, Co. Meath, which was held on the first Sunday in

August. This was described by Wilde as

'one of the most beautiful holy wells in Ireland and shaded by a hoary ash tree of surpassing size and beauty.'

The ash tree is no longer there, but the well is still famous. It was produced by a miracle of St. Ciaran and it cures almost every disease, backache, headache and even toothache. The power of the water is greatly increased at midnight before the pattern day, the first Sunday of August, and this increase lasts for an hour, and to a less extent, for a further twenty-three hours. The well has even got sacred trout, which can only be seen for a short time after midnight on the festival day, and at midnight the pilgrims use many lights in their efforts to catch a glimpse of the sacred fish.

Some other Lughnasa pilgrimages may be mentioned; one is to St. Brigid's Well in Brideswell village, Co. Roscommon, and another is at St. Brigid's Well at Liscannor, Co. Clare. This last was described by Shaw-Mason early in the nineteenth century:

On Saturday evening, preceding this Sunday numbers of people male and female assemble at St. Bridget's Well and remain there the entire of the night. They first perform their rounds and then spend a good part of the time in invoking this St. Bridget over the well, repeating their prayers and adorations aloud and holding their conversations with the saint etc. When this ceremony is over they amuse themselves until morning by dancing and singing.

In the Irish calendar, some feast days are found on August 1st. One of these is St. Dervla, whose well, known as Dabhach Daerbhle, is at the southern tip of the Mullet peninsula in Co. Mayo. A Pattern was held at this well until it was stopped by the parish priest there, Dr. Lyons, and a well, dedicated to St. Dervla, was also visited on a small island, South Iniskea, off the Mayo coast. O'Donovan also mentioned a Tobar Deirbhill in Dunfeeney parish in Co. Mayo. In Kildavan parish in Co. Wexford, a pattern was once held at St. Davan's Well on the 1st of August.

The 29th of September, the feast of St. Michael the Archangel, was also a popular day and many of the saint's wells are found. Perhaps the best known is one at Ballinskelligs in Co. Kerry, which was described by Smith. This may have derived some of its reputation from the ancient monastic site on Skellig Michael, off the Kerry coast, to which there once was a pilgrimage, but this appears to have been discontinued by the eighteenth century. A holy well

St. Brigid's Well, Liscannor, Co. Clare. Entrance to the well house. Votive offerings on right.

near St. Mullins in Co. Carlow was mentioned by O'Toole. It was dedicated to St. Michael and visited on his feast day and O'Toole also mentioned the custom of preparing and eating mutton pasties on this feast day. Other wells dedicated to St. Michael and visited on his feast day are recorded from Belclare parish, Co. Galway, in Charlestown parish, Co. Louth, and in St. Michael's parish, Co. Wexford, where O'Donovan says that people continued to visit the well after the pattern had been stopped.

The fourth of the great festivals of the ancient Celts, Samhain, is the festival of the end of autumn and coincides with our present Hallow Eve – All Saints Day. It was not a time of year suitable for an assembly in the open air and there are few pilgrimages around this time. The pilgrimage to the holy well and graveyard at All Saints near Banaher, Co. Offaly ends on the 1st of November, but this appears to be a modern practice. All Saints Well between Cork and Blarney was visited on All Saints Day and on the following Sunday and a writer in the *Journal of the Cork Historical and Archaeological Society* said that the well was covered by a stone building with the date 1761. In Smarmour parish, Co. Louth, a pattern was held on All Saints Day.

Some other pilgrimages around this time may have begun as Samhain festivals. St. Coleman's Well in Colmanswell parish, Co.

Limerick, was visited on the 29th of October, and in Ughtama parish, a holy well dedicated to St. Colman Mac Duach is also known as Sruthan-na-Naomh and was visited on the 5th of November. In Co. Mayo, a well called Tobar Adhlain in Kilconickny parish was visited on the 31st of October, when a pattern was held.

The last popular feast day was the 11th of November, the feast of St. Martin. On this day, it was the custom to kill some animal from a bullock down to a cock, depending on the wealth of the individual or the size of his household. Wells dedicated to St. Martin are found near Shillelagh, Co. Wicklow, in Cloghane parish in Co. Kerry and in Noughaval parish, Co. Clare.

IV

Legends of Holy Wells

If it is necessary to define what is a holy well, it may be said that a holy well is any collection of water which for one reason or another is considered to be holy. Often there is a story to explain why the well is believed to be holy. These stories are of all ages: some are derived from the prechristian mythology of the race, and others came into being during the eighteenth or even during the nineteenth century. In some cases the well and its holiness are attributed to the powers of the saint, who may have caused it to appear miraculously or he may have overcome and displaced his enemies, whom he found in charge of the well.

The most famous of all these stories may be that one which concerns the origin of the River Boyne. The river rises in a pool, now known as Trinity Well, near Carbury, Co. Kildare, and at present a popular pilgrimage is made to this well on Trinity Sunday. The story is that a king called Nechtan lived at Carbury Hill, known in Irish as Sídh Nechtain, and had in his garden a very special well, which no woman might approach. Despite this, Boan, the wife of Nechtan, not only approached the well, but insulted it gravely by walking three times round it in an anti-clockwise direction. At the insult the well rose and chased her, as she fled screaming, so forming the River Boyne. Eventually the water overtook her and swept her out to sea, where she was drowned.

The prechristian Irish worshipped the River Boyne as a goddess and clearly this story is derived from their religious beliefs. Wilde in his book on the Boyne mentions a number of other holy wells which are found close to the young river, and add their waters to it. These are now as completely christianised as Trinity Well. The first is Tobercro (Tobar Croiche Naoimh – The Well of the Holy Cross). Wilde then mentioned The Beautiful Well and next to it Lady Well, where he said that a pattern was held early in the nineteenth century. In a recent visit (1974) I could not hear of any tradition of

48

this. Wilde also mentioned two others, Carbury Well and Tobar na Cille – 'six in all, baptizing the infant Boyne.'

A similar story is recorded about the Origin of Loch Gamhna on the Cavan-Longford border. The head of Loch Gamhna is a holy well in Rathbracken townland, in Columcille parish, Co. Longford. The story says that once, long long ago, a woman profaned the well by washing dirty clothes in it. As a consequence of the insult a calf, which lived at the bottom of the well, jumped out and ran towards the valley which is now filled by Loch Gamhna and, as could be expected, the water rose and followed the calf and so formed the lake under which the supernatural calf now lives.

This story, in one form or other, is told about many Irish lakes. The best known of these is that one told about Loch Neagh, but the first time I heard it the story was about a small lake in Fenagh parish in Co. Leitrim. This was known as 'the Clear Lake' and contained very pleasant tasting spring water, and over the greater part of it, it was possible to see the bottom. The story was of a well which contained wonderful water, but everyone who drew water from it must immediately replace the cover on the well. Once when a woman forgot or neglected to do this, the well rose and followed her and as she fled in terror she passed a man who was mowing grass with a scythe. The man, realising what had happened, cut her legs off with the scythe, and left her lying on the ground, while he hurried to safety. When I asked why he had done this, it was explained that if he had not done it, the water would have continued to spread until it had covered the whole country.

Another prechristian story tells of the origin of a number of holy wells in Ballyboy (Kilcormack) parish, Co. Offaly. John O'Donovan was told that one of St. Cormac's fellow saints had prophesied that he (Cormac) would be attacked and killed by wolves. In order to make sure that this prophecy would not be fulfilled Cormac built a tower in which there was no opening, except at the top through which the necessaries of life were passed to him. One evening as he sat looking out through the opening, he saw two black snails creeping up the wall towards him. As they came towards him the snails appeared to change their forms and, realising the danger, he threw himself out of the tower and ran pursued by the snails who had now become a pair of savage wolves. As he ran he fell in a number of places, and in each place a fountain of clear water sprang out of the ground, until finally the wolves caught him, and tore him to pieces.

Tullaghan Well, Co. Sligo, has been famous since the twelfth century, when it was mentioned by Gerald Barry, among the

Wonders of Ireland. Barry said that the well was on the top of a high mountain and far from the coast, yet its waters ebb and flow like the tides of the sea. This belief continued until modern times, and the fact that the water was slightly brackish, was taken as proof that it was connected with the sea. There are two legends, each of which is said to explain the origin of this well. One says that St. Patrick, having defeated the demons of Cruach Patrick, chased one of them, called Caorthannach from the Reek to Tullaghan, and as she fled she polluted all the wells and the saint became very thirsty. At Tullaghan he prayed and the well appeared, so he was able to drink. An older story says that Gam, the servant of Eremon, one of the leaders of the Goedelic Celts, was killed on Slieve Gamh and his head was cast into the well.

The fact that there are three prehistoric cashels on the hill where the well is would indicate that this may have been a prechristian well and the legends would agree with this suggestion. Added to these is the fact that the well was visited on the first Sunday of August, the prechristian festival of Lughnasa.

In Manus O'Donnell's *Life of St. Columcille* there is a story of a well in the land called Pictoria. This was what it said:

If anyone washed hands or feet or drank the water he became blind, deaf and afflicted with leprosy, or paralysis, or other foul distemper. The druids and devils did it, and people honoured the well. When Columcille came to the well the druids were glad because they believed it would harm him. St. Columcille blessed the well, and washed his hands and feet in it, and drank the water, and ever since the well hath healed every malady, and distemper that hath drawn nigh it.

A similar story is told, in less colourful language, about St. Patrick's Well at Granard Cille, Co. Longford. It is said that when Patrick came to the district he first defeated the druids of Carbury, who were in charge of the well. Then, having won, he blessed the well and ever since it has been honoured as holy.

In the *Tripartite Life of St. Patrick* there is a story of the saint's visit to Cruachan, where the kings of Connacht lived. The saint with his companions came to the well called Clebach, which was at the east of Cruachan and there at sunrise they met the daughters of the High King, who came to the well to wash 'after the Custom of Women.' The saint spoke to them and told them about his mission and baptised them, with water from a well. During a recent (1975) visit to Tulsk in Co. Roscommon I learned of a local belief that Tobar Oguila near Tulsk is the well called Clebach, and people used visit it on St. Patrick's Day. It is now visited on a Sunday in June, and Mass is said at the well.

In some of the legends the enemy is called 'a great serpent' (*Oll Phiast*), and in a story about the origin of Tobar Barry in Co. Roscommon the Oll Phiast lived on a neighbouring hill called Slieve Badhan, near Strokestown. When St. Barry came, he attacked the Oll Phiast and chased it towards Lough Lagan, where it plunged in and disappeared for ever. Before it disappeared, the saint thrust at it with his crozier, the *Gearr Barry*, and at the spot where his knee touched the ground, a well sprang up. St. Barry then blessed the well 'and it retains his blessing to this day'.

This story of a contest between saint and serpent is told in many of the Lives of Irish Saints. St. Kevin, when he came to Glendalough, was able to displace a serpent which lived in the Upper Lake and did harm to men and beasts, but the saint moved it to the Lower Lake, where it did no further harm.

In the *Ordnance Survey Letters* from Co. Kerry, O'Donovan told of St. Connla who killed a great serpent, which lived at Lisnapeasta in Kilconly parish.

Some of these stories may contain a few grains of historical truth, and it is probable that some of the wells were considered holy by the prechristian Irish. From the little we know of the religion of the Celts, it is certain that wells and other natural features were considered sacred. A well-known modern authority, Professor Myles Dillon, wrote:

'One of the most fundamental features of Gaulish religion is the wide prevalence of sanctuaries, connected with natural features especially springs, rivers, lakes and forests.'

During the second half of the fifth century, when Christianity was displacing paganism in Ireland the conflict between the old and the new may have been fought out near the sacred wells or in the sacred groves. The sign of the victory of the saint was that he blessed the well and used the water to baptise the new Christians. It is easy to create imaginary pictures of what may have taken place but such imagining does not help in studying the origin of the wells. A credible story in the Life of St. Loman says that the saint came to Trim on the Boyne. There he met the local ruler 'and there being an open fountain in that place he was baptised in Christ by Loman.' This may have been what happened, in reality, rather than the dramatic stories about the druids and great serpents.

On Valentia Island, one of the holy wells there is called Tober – olla – Breanainn (The Well of St. Brendan's Anointing). The story is that St. Brendan, while passing the island in a boat was summoned to give baptism to two dying men. He landed and climbed the cliff, aided by a miraculous set of steps and was guided by a stranger to where the dying men were. The stranger then disappeared. Brendan used the water of the well to perform the baptisms, and ever since it has been a holy well.

Another famous Co. Kerry well is Tober na Mult (Well of the Wethers) in the parish of Ardfert, and there are two stories to explain why the well is so named. One says that the wethers were the fee given to Bishop Erc for baptising St. Brendan. A later and more imaginative story tells of a priest whose enemies were hunting him with the aid of bloodhounds. As the priest came to the well three wethers jumped out of it and were followed by the hounds and the hunters, leaving the priest safe.

In the south of the old graveyard at Kilroot, Co. Antrim, there is a holy well. This is attributed to St. Ailbe who landed there from the sea and founded a church. Unfortunately there was no water conveniently available so Ailbe blessed a stone from which water began to flow, and then the saint said 'though it is small it will never fail'. Tober Moling at Mullinakill, in Rosbercon parish, Co. Kilkenny, is well known because its waters are used to treat ulcers of the skin. This power was given to it by St. Moling, who himself suffered from such ulcers and used the water to cure them. At St. Mullins in Co. Carlow a part of the pilgrimage was that the pilgrims should walk in the bed of a small stream there against the current. This was done because it was said St. Moling made a water course to bring water to his monastery, and when the work was finished Moling waded in the water against the current. This was a famous pilgrimage during the Middle Ages and the practice continued until the nineteenth century.

In the *Life of St. Columcille* there is mention of the healing power of the water of a well called Tobar an Deilg (Well of the Thorn). It says that Columcille had a thorn in his foot which he bathed in the well and as a result the thorn came out. Ever since people with thorns go to the well and bathe the part. The well was at Caerthe Snamha on the east side of Lough Foyle, but it does not appear to be remembered at present.

There is a legend about the origin of St. Laserian's well at Old Leighlin. It appears that when the saint was building his church there, the workmen were greatly helped by a wonderful bullock which pulled the cart of stones to the site. Each evening the bullock was killed to feed the workers, and was found alive and well the next morning, but St. Laserian warned them sternly that they must not injure any of the bones of the animal. One morning it was seen to be lame, and the man who had injured the bone of the animal's leg got ulcers. In terror he went to the saint and told what he had done, and Laserian, with a gentleness not characteristic of Irish saints, forgave him. In addition he caused a well to appear and told the man to bathe the ulcers in the water. The well is still known as a healing well. This story is also told about the parish of Errigal – Kerry, in Co. Tyrone. In this case the bones were each night put in St. Ciaran's Well. Here the culprit, a man called MacMahon, provoked the wrath of the saint who prophesied that before the church was finished the top would fall on a MacMahon.

At Ardagh in Co. Longford it is said that St. Brigid was there before St. Patrick came. When Patrick arrived, Brigid, in order to demonstrate her prowess as a miracle worker before the great man, carried a live coal in her apron and in the spot where she dropped it the holy well sprang up. For a well with such a distinguished beginning it is a poor one which often runs dry during the summer.

There are many wells in the country which are noted for their power to cure diseases of the eyes. One of these, in the parish of Kilkeerin in Co. Roscommon, was visited by John O'Donovan, who recorded the story of its origin. The local saint was the virgin St. Caolainn and it happened that a man told her that he admired her eyes. When the saint heard this she gouged out her eyes, threw them on the ground and said 'there they are for you.' She then groped her way to a place in a townland called Moor, where she found a tuft of rushes. She pulled up two of the rushes and caused a well to appear, and when she had bathed her eye sockets with the water her sight was restored. The water continued to cure sore eyes for a thousand years, until an enemy (Protestant) washed a child in the well. At this insult the well moved to another site some distance away, leaving in its place a deep hole in which no water is ever seen to collect.

There are many versions of this story heard in different parts of the country, and in at least three cases St. Brigid is the heroine. One of these is told of a well in Killinagh parish in Co. Cavan and another about a well at Dunleer, Co. Louth. It is also told about St. Brigid's Well at Faughart, also in Co. Louth. Probably this legend is based on Our Lord's advice 'If thy right eye scandalize thee pluck it out' but no Irish saint would ever be satisfied with such a half measure, as only plucking out one eye.

A story is told about two wells on the seashore at Flodigarry on the Isle of Skye. Once, long ago, the Christians and the Pagans of the district quarrelled about the use of the local well, so they appealed to St. Turog, who lived in Flodigarry Island, to settle the dispute. The saint agreed, but when he came to arbitrate, he found that the parties had again begun to fight, so he struck the well with his *bachall* and it became dry. He then returned to his island. Before long the parties, now very crestfallen at the anger of the saint and the loss of their well, went again to Flodigarry and begged him once more to come and help them. He returned and first separated the parties. Then he struck the ground in front of one group and then in front of the other group, causing two wells of good clear water to appear.

St. Brigid's Well near Cliffony in Co. Sligo was formerly visited on 1st February. The story here is that St. Brigid used to pray while immersed in the water, even in the coldest weather. Once when she came to the well to pray, she found it dry and it continued dry until she was persuaded to stop the practice of having cold baths.

It is often said that St. Ciaran of Saigher preached Christianity in Ireland before St. Patrick. The legend is that Ciaran met Patrick in Rome and Patrick decided to send him to Ireland as his precursor. Before Ciaran left, Patrick told him to go to a well in Ireland and begin his work there, but Ciaran very reasonably pointed out that there were many wells in Ireland and asked how should he recognise the well which Patrick meant. Patrick then gave Ciaran a bell and assured him that it would not ring until he came to where the special well was. The bell rang when Ciaran reached Saigher, so he established his monastery there. When later Patrick reached Ireland, and came to Saigher to visit his friend, Ciaran changed the water of the well into wine to welcome him.

A similar guide bell story is told of St. Mochua of Balla who, when he left Bangor, took a bell to guide him to Tehelly. The bell, however, insisted on guiding him to Balla in Co. Mayo, where he settled and built his church.

Jocelyn in his *Life of St. Patrick* told a story of St. Patrick's Well at Nassau Street, Dublin. It seems that when St. Patrick came there the people told him that all the water in the local wells was brackish, so the saint prayed and gave them a well of good sweet water.

It would not be difficult to tell many more stories about the origin of holy wells, and of how and why, the water has acquired its powers. Quite clearly they are not true, but the essential point is that they have been told for hundreds of years, and similar stories can be heard in many other countries. Many of them suggest a memory of the time when Christianity was replacing the older religion, and it may have been that the struggle was sterner and more prolonged than is said in school history books. This of course is a problem for scholars – real scholars. Here it is not proper to attempt to draw any

St. Patrick's Well is in the grounds of Trinity College Dublin, underneath the Nassau Street entrance. It is said that in about 1700 a certain Dr. Gwither placed frogspawn in this well, and by this means brought frogs to Ireland. See p. 54.

conclusions but, limited and obscure as the evidence is, it does indicate that in visiting and praying at holy wells we are doing something which has been done for thousands of years, and goes back long before Christianity to the origin of the race.

All over the country stories are told about the origin of lakes and these are often associated with threats of death and danger. Examples of these are stories of the Snail Well, the waters of which will overwhelm Sligo town, and stories of the powerful and often malevolent lady, called Aillfhion, who gave her name to Loch Allen. If one goes on Loch Allen in a boat it is unwise to speak disrespectfully of her because if she is displeased she is likely to raise a sudden storm on the lake. Loch Allen is notable for its sudden storms.

There are many legends about a supernatural cow called the Glas Gaibhleann which is often associated with holy wells, and some wells are called Tobar na Glaise. This cow is associated with three wells in Co. Sligo, one in Donegal and one in Co. Cavan. The story is that the wonderful cow gave milk to all who needed it, until some-one annoyed or insulted her, so she departed and was seen no more. Another supernatural cow called the Bo Finne gives her name to Inisbofinne off the Donegal coast, and to another Island of the White Cow off the Mayo coast. Here she used to be seen coming from the little lake on the island.

V

The Position of the Well

Some people may feel disappointed at the sight of one of these holy wells. It may have been a famous well for centuries, and the visitor is probably expecting to see something unusual, but instead he is taken to what looks like a drinking pool for cattle which in a dry summer might be nothing more than a muddy puddle. He may sometimes find that the 'holy well' is not a well at all. It may be a deep pool in a stream, or a waterfall, or a collection of rain water in a hollow stone. It may be a small lake, or even a pool of water which is found in a hollow tree stump. Some of the wells are found in interesting places and in many cases one can hear stories to explain why the well has come to be thought holy.

SEASHORE WELLS

Some holy wells are found on the seashore near to the high water mark, and in a number of cases the well is found between the tide levels. On the strand at Ardmore, Co. Waterford, there are three such wells which have been attributed to a miracle of St. Declan. At present it is very difficult to find these wells and they can only be reached at very low spring tides. I have been told that this is due to recent coast erosion, but it was difficult to find them about the year 1836, when Philip Dixon Hardy described the pilgrimage. It is firmly believed that the water of these wells will cure all internal complaints.

O'Curry in the *Ordnance Survey Letters* from Co. Clare described a seashore well in Moyarta parish. He wrote:

> One furlong east of Teampull-an-Aird in Kilcradaun townland at the bottom of a cliff in the very face of the headland is the fresh water holy well of St. Cradaun, ranking among the most popular wells in Ireland for the cure of all diseases but more especially

57

diseases of the eyes and limbs. The well is sunk in the solid rock, and is overflown by the salt sea at every full tide but the moment the tide recedes the water in the well is as pure and fresh as ever. There is a small cave or recess in the cliff behind it, in which people are in the habit of spending whole nights in prayer in fulfilment of vows made in times of danger from sickness or drowning etc. On the bank above this well there is a large heap of small stones and pebbles deposited there by the votaries while performing the *turras*.

O'Donovan tells of another tidal well, this one dedicated to St. Finan in Kenmare parish, Co. Kerry. The ruined church is about a mile south east of the little town and the holy well is a hundred paces from the church. He says that at high water during spring tides the salt water gets into the well. Patterns were held there on the 3rd of May and on the 14th of September but these were abolished about the year 1820. Despite this the people continued to visit the well and do the stations and it was said that many diseases were cured by 'the said waters.' Also in Co. Kerry in Minard parish the old church was dedicated to Our Lady. One hundred yards east of the church on the seashore there is a holy well dedicated to St. John the Baptist. Formerly a pattern had been held there on 29th August.

A number of these seashore wells can be found on the coast of Co. Dublin. One of these is Tobar Caillin near Rush. It was described by Dr. Kevin Danaher as 'a small hollow into which water trickles from a spring in the cliff bank over the sea close to high tide mark.' There is another one, St. Mochuda's Well at Bunnow which is reached by the sea at some high spring tides. Although this well is no longer visited by pilgrims, there was formerly a popular pattern held there on Lammas Sunday and the water was used to treat whooping cough. Near the Martello Tower at Carrickhill, Portmarnock, there is a holy well called Tobar MacLarney. In this case the water comes out of the sand on the foreshore and picnickers who knew where to look could find fresh water when the tide was out. Near Blackrock at Newtown, Tobernea was also a seashore well. This was a strong trickle of water which flowed down the face of a rock. It was close to the sea until the railway embankment was built there.

The best known of this group of Co. Dublin wells is the 'Chink Well' near Portrane. The well is in a cave on the seashore, and at each high tide the cave is filled and the well covered with sea water. As its name implies (Chincough) the well is reputed to cure whooping cough and many votive offerings were left by pilgrims, to be swept out to sea by the tide. One description of the well, in the *Ulster Journal of Archaeology*, said that people seeking a cure of whooping cough, used to leave pieces of bread as votive offerings and if it was seen that the bread was carried out to sea by the tide the prognosis was thought to be favourable.

On the coast of Co. Antrim between Whitehead and Black Head there is a famous seashore holy well. This was described in detail in the *Ulster Journal of Archaeology*. The writer says that the well is among rocks on the seashore and is 'covered at full tide for a fortnight every month yet the water is always wholesome.' He quotes R. Dobbs' description of Co. Antrim, which was written in 1683.

> At the White Head in the parish of Broad Island at Temple Corran there is a spring well which runs very plentifully out of the limestone rocks into the sea: not to be seen at low [sic] water! Much frequented by the neighbouring people on May Eve yearly.

Morris, in a very comprehensive article on the holy wells of Co. Donegal, describes a large number of these seashore wells. One of these, dedicated to St. Patrick, may be found near to the ruins of Assaroe Abbey at Ballyshannon. Shaw Mason in his account of the Parish of Kilbarron said that the well was visited on the last Sunday of July. It was a well of 'very fine spring water near the ruins of the Abbey of Ashrow: to the sanctity of which however the spring tides flowing over it pay no particular regard.'

In *JRSAI* we get some more details about this ancient well. It bubbled out from a hollow of the rock several feet below high water mark and was called Tobar na Boghilla. It was visited, the writer said, between 1st and 15th of August and the neighbouring bushes were covered with rags. Near the well was 'a natural cavern, probably in some measure sculptured out by the hand of man' and it was believed that St. Patrick used the cave as a baptistry and a chapel. At the east end of this cave there was an altar like shelf on which there were two *bullans*.

Malin Well near Malin Head is a famous holy well and has been described many times since Dr. Thomas Molyneux wrote about it in 1708: 'Here the sick come from all parts to be cured by going into it.' As at Assaroe there is a cave in the cliff nearby and this is known as the 'Wee House of Malin.' People say 'it holds all that goes into it and the more that goes into it the more it holds.' The well was a natural basin which was filled at each high tide, and many of the references to it were quoted in the Donegal Annual in 1970.

Not far from Malin Well are what are called Cathal Dubh's three boiling wells at the Black Rock, at Strabreaghy. They are three little bubbling springs on the left hand side of the road from Carndonagh to Malin in Drumaville townland and are covered by the sea at high tide. It is said that Cathal Dubh was a hermit who lived in the neighbourhood.

A few miles away near Clonmany there is another seashore well which is covered at high tide. This one appears to have been dedicated to St. Columcille and was visited on his feast day, the 9th of June. Morris heard that on that day people used drive their cattle between the well and the shore and swim them in the tide, to render them immune to disease.

Morris also mentions a seashore well at Anney in Rath Mullan parish which he says is reached by the tide and is visited by people suffering from headaches. Another one, called Eas Fionnain, is south of Dunfanaghy, on the edge of the sea. O'Donovan gave a dramatic description of the visit which he paid to it on a wet windy day, while his companion shirked the dangerous cliff path down to the sea. Pilgrims visited the well on the first Monday of each quarter and on 15th August when they made ten rounds of the well.

A holy well of somewhat doubtful reputation is at Cnoc Fola at the north west corner of the Irish coast. It is called Tobar Faoi Cnoc, or Tobar Alt na Peiste, but it does not appear ever to have had the name of any saint given to it. The well is covered by the tide twice daily and the path which leads to it is both difficult and dangerous. There was a very famous seashore well on an island called Inis-bofinne between Tory and the mainland. At present the island is uninhabited and the well, Tobar Gas Columcille, has been eroded by the sea in recent years.

Some inland holy wells are found in places where they may sometimes be covered by the waters of a neighbouring lake or river. St. Finian's Well at Clonmacnoise is visited as part of the pilgrimage but sometimes it may be covered by the waters of the River Shannon, and at other times during the summer the well may be found dry. In November 1975 I visited Tobar Ogulla near Tulsk in Co. Roscommon. I noticed that the water of a stream flowing beside the well might easily overflow into it, and I was able to learn that this often happened during wet weather. Some wells are found on lake shores, and might easily be covered by flood waters. It is at present rather difficult to judge this because the levels of many lakes have been lowered by drainage schemes, but Lassair Well beside Lough Mealey in Co. Roscommon might still be reached by the lake water during winter floods.

It would appear that there was some special significance attached to these wells which were covered by the tide, and whose sacred

The holy well near Lacken, Co. Wicklow. It was covered by water when the Poulaphuca Lakes were formed. When at the end of summer 1978 the level of the water was lowered people went to the well in large numbers. The walls shown were built about 1880 because people bathed in the water. On a Sunday in November 1978 I saw over 3,000 people there.

water drained into the sea. It is not clear what our ancestors believed about this but it is possible to guess. In the case of a famous well on Inish Murray it was formerly the custom to draw the well in order to calm the sea or to provide a favourable wind, and there was a similar practice at a well on the shore of Teelin Bay, Co. Donegal. It may have been believed that the water of the holy well added to the sea caused storms to cease. Or it may have been thought to increase the catches of fish.

Near some of these seashore wells there are remains of ancient churches. This would be expected but in at least three cases there are caves near the wells. The three are those at Kilcradaun in Co. Clare, and at Malin Well and the holy well at Assaroe Abbey, both in Donegal. In each of these cases the pilgrims appear to have prayed and spent some time in the caves. The Chink Well at Portrane, Co. Dublin, is itself in a cave, but I found no tradition that pilgrims prayed there.

MOUNTAIN TOP AND HILL TOP WELLS

Some holy wells are found on, or very near, the tops of mountains or hills. To a person who knew nothing about impermeable layers of rock such hill top wells would seem to be due to a supernatural power and might have been thought holy long before Christianity came to Ireland. In some cases these mountain top wells became famous places of pilgrimage, but they often retain evidence of prechristian beliefs and practices, and sometimes the Christian veneer is thin.

The most dramatic of these mountain top wells is found on the summit of Mount Brandon (3127 feet) on the Dingle Peninsula in Co. Kerry. The well dedicated to St. Brendan is close to a small oratory called Teampuilin Breannain, and near it are a few small mounds called 'the graves' and a pillar stone called *Leac na nDrom*. The climb is especially difficult from the east side and is beyond the ability of many ordinary people, so that despite a spectacular effort to revive it in 1868 its popularity has declined. Formerly, people made the pilgrimage on May 16th St. Brendan's Day, and on June 29th, the feast of St. Peter and St. Paul, but the most popular day was the last Sunday of July, and it has been identified by Mac Neill as a Lughnasa festival site.

It was the custom to climb the mountain during the night but the older practice was to do this on the previous evening, during daylight and spend the night on the mountain before beginning the rounds shortly after daybreak. The pilgrims first prayed at the little ruined church and then walked round it. They then went round Leac na nDrom and then circled 'the graves.' This ritual was repeated nine times as the rosary was recited, and the pilgrims ended by drinking some of the water of the well. Those who sought a cure for backache then stood with their backs against Leac na nDrom. The pilgrims then went down to the village of Cloghane where a pattern was held on the same day.

This was once a famous pilgrimage. There are references to it in the medieval *Lives of St. Brendan* and in documents of the fourteenth and sixteenth centuries. The many legends however that are told about the district show that the pilgrimage is older than Christianity.

Another notable mountain well is on the top of Slieve League in Co. Donegal. O'Donovan mentioned the holy well beside the little church of St. Aodh Mac Bric to which pilgrimages were made on the 10th November. The route to the mountain top is difficult and dangerous and might only be undertaken by intrepid mountaineers.

O'Donovan continued:

> On the summit of the gloomy mountain of Slieve Laig are yet shown the ruins of the little cell of Aodh Mac Bric . . . and a holy well blessed by him. A most solemn *turas* was performed here in the memory of the last generation but he liveth not now who could point out all the hallowed spots to be visited, and prayed at, so that it has been abandoned as a station of pilgrimage.

O'Donovan quoted Colgan's *Life of Aidus the son of Breccius* (Aodh Mac Bric)

> 'he is venerated . . . in Sliabh Liag in Tir Connell where a chapel is consecrated to him, and a solemn pilgrimage performed.'

This reference to the pilgrimage to the top of Slieve League was written in the first half of the seventeenth century.

Slieve Sneacht (2019 feet) in Inishowen is another site of a mountain top well. Here the story is that St. Patrick prayed and fasted on Slieve Sneacht for forty days as he is said to have done on Cruach Patrick. O'Donovan himself climbed to the top but failed to find the well which was known as Tobar na Suil and was visited on the Sunday before the 26th July. It is thought unwise to stir up the mud in the bottom of the well because on the way back down the mountainside mist, rain or snow, may fall.

Two other famous mountain top wells may be mentioned. These are the well on the top of Slieve Donard (2796 feet) the highest point in the Mourne Mountains, and the well on the top of Church Mountain on the west side of the Wicklow Mountains. These have been discussed in detail by Mac Neill who has identified each of them as Lughnasa festival sites.

There are less dramatic hill top wells which are centres of famous pilgrimages. One of these is Croc a' Loch, near Malin Head, where a small lake on the 800 foot contour line is considered holy and dedicated to St. Patrick. Henry Morris says that there is no special day or time to do the *turras*, but people go fasting and walk round the lake three times. In this case the story is that St. Patrick drove two monsters and a spotted horse out of the lake and as proof of the truth of this story, an outline of the monsters and horse may be made out on the eastern slope of Picture Hill near the lake. Another hill top well described by Morris in Co. Donegal is Tobar na Suil on the top of Cnoc a' Toighe south of Churchill near Gartan Lake. The story is that St. Columcille, when pursued by his enemies, leaped from the hill top to a great rock some distance away where he left his footprints, and as part of the truth of the story the footprints can still be seen. There is still another of these wells on the top of Derryreel hill four miles east of Falcaragh.

O'Donovan described a well dedicated to St. John the Baptist in Drumcullin parish, Offaly. The well is at the top of Knockbarron Hill, which is a short distance south west of what is called St. John's Rock. The well has been reopened during this century and the pilgrimage is performed, as expected, on St. John's Eve., i.e. Midsummer Day. Mac Neill described a pilgrimage to a holy well on the top of Downpatrick Head in Co. Mayo, which is also a Lughnasa festival.

Mac Allister in 1896 described a holy well, on Ard Oilean, a small island off the coast of Connemara, the water of which was said to cure colic and other such complaints. The well is found near the highest point in the island and it is clear that the water in the well could not have drained into it.

As has been said many of these mountain and hill top wells appear to have been part of the prechristian religion of the Irish. The fact that a well of good water, or any well at all, was found on the top of a mountain or hill would be a cause for wonder and would certainly be attributed to some supernatural cause. Similarly the well of fresh water found at the highest point of Ard Oilean must have been thought of as supernatural: no other explanation would be possible to the ancient Irish.

BOG WELLS

It would be a cause for wonder if a well of good fresh water could be found springing from a bog. Such a well was described by John O'Donovan in the parish of Taghmaconnell in Co. Roscommon, and as usual there is a story about a miracle of the saint, to explain the presence of the well. It was said that one of St. Ciaran's converts, a certain Carbry Crom, was killed by his enemies, who cut off his head. Carbry was restored to life by St. Ciaran, but in replacing the head the saint did not put it on straight. Near the well there is an ancient cross, called the Cross of Carbury Crom, which was said to have been erected to commemorate the miracle. As a sort of encore St. Ciaran caused 'a fountain of living water' to gush from the bog.

On Valencia Island, Co. Kerry, there is a holy well called Tobar Olla Breannain, which was described in the *Kerry Archaeological Journal*. It also is found in an area of soft bogland and in this case the story tells how St. Brendan used the water to baptize a dying man.

In one of the *Ordnance Survey Letters* from Co. Clare, O'Curry described Tobar Ghraine in Feacle parish

It is in the centre of a bog three miles from Feacle. It is five feet square surrounded by stones placed on their edges and covered by a large horizontal flagstone 8' × 7'6" which covers it leaving in a small hole in the west end. Just as in the Book of Armagh.

Clearly this is a very special well and its power to cure sore eyes was only one of many powers which it may have possessed.

Still another bog well is Tobar Mac Duach in Oranmore parish, Co. Galway, which was mentioned by O'Donovan.

MOUNTAIN PASS WELLS

Some holy wells are found at the tops of mountain passes – natural meeting places for people from either side of the mountain. Perhaps the best known of these wells is one dedicated to St. Patrick, which can be found at the top of a pass called Mám Éan (1200 feet), leading from the Joyce country southward to Connemara proper, in Co. Galway. The most notable of the legends attached to this well tells that St. Patrick, having passed through the Joyce country, climbed to the top of Mám where he stopped, looked down on Connemara, gave it his blessing, but did not continue on into it.

This is a famous well, and the pilgrimage and the pattern were described a number of times. One nineteenth century visitor wrote in the *Journal of the Royal Society of Antiquaries*,

Walk a mile from Recess Hotel towards the Outerard road. The road turns left towards the mountains for another mile, then a poor track up to the top of the Pass, and the well is at the top. A loose circle of stones is around it, on which old jam crocks are to be seen. There is a rude wooden cross in the circle at the well. St. Patrick's Bed, rather like St. Kevin's at Glendalough, is cut out of a rock cliff on the west side of the pass and a little higher up than the well.

This well which is visited on the last Sunday of July has been identified by Mac Neill as a Lughnasa festival site.

Another such well was described by Morris. This is at the top of the Pass of Mamore, which leads from the west side of Lough Swilly to the interior of Inishowen. The pass reaches a height of 900 feet and runs between Mamore Hill (1381 feet) and Ueris (1379 feet). The well is visited on 15th August and the pilgrims go round seven cairns in their bare feet before finishing at the well.

CHURCH WELLS

In the great majority of cases the holy well can be found close to the ruins of the medieval parish church, or to the ruins of some other ancient church. In some cases the remains of the church may have long disappeared, and been forgotten, but there may be an old graveyard close to the well or in some cases a *Cillin* may be found. Sometimes a story will be told about the local saint and often the well has a part in the story. It may have been the scene of some of his many miracles or it may have been created miraculously at his command. These wells are usually mentioned in the *Ordnance Survey Letters*. They may be found north south east or west of the church site, but within a short distance of it, and it may be suggested, despite the legends, that most of them began as the source of the domestic water supply for the church.

The ordinary reason why a church is built is to provide for the spiritual needs of the people of the neighbourhood. It is therefore likely that it would be built close to some centre of population and when it had been built people would tend to come and live near the church. It will also be remembered that in medieval Ireland the church was the administrative centre of the parish. In gaelic Ireland the *airchinneach* who held the church lands and might be thought of as the lay administrator of the parish, probably lived near the church. Often there was a *teach aoidh* (house of hospitality) in the parish, and normally this was convenient to the church. All the church property which was administered by the *airchinneach* would be thought of as the property of the local saint, and this would include the local well.

The custom of making pilgrimages to the saint's well is very old but the practice may have become more widespread during the seventeenth and eighteenth centuries. When the Church of Ireland, the Established Church, took control of the parish churches people generally ceased to attend the services, if any were held, but they continued to use the old burial ground, and in some parishes this custom is still continued. It may have been that this was when the practice spread and would explain why during the eighteenth century some well houses were built and other work was done at the wells.

In any case by the eighteenth century, when many of the old churches had become ruinous and had been abandoned, the custom of visiting the holy well could be found in most parishes in the country. The most valuable source of information about these church wells is the *Ordnance Survey Letters* written by John

O'Donovan and his colleagues shortly before the great famine. The Co. Clare letters written mainly by Eoghan O'Curry, himself a Clareman, are very informative and in them he gave the position of forty of these wells. Of the forty, twenty-three were convenient to the ruins of the old parish churches, and seven were close to old disused graveyards or to the sites of other old churches. In ten cases, as far as one could learn from the letters, the well was not near the site of any old church. The letters from Galway, Mayo, Sligo, Leitrim and Cavan, are much the same. In these areas roughly two-thirds of the wells are close to the sites of the old churches. Even in such areas as Co. Louth and Co. Waterford the holy wells are found close to the old churches, and these counties had been under Norman and English influence ever since the thirteenth century.

It seems reasonable to suggest therefore that the majority of the holy wells began as the source of water for the few people who lived near the church. This question could only be further investigated by people who knew each district in detail and without this knowledge it is unwise to speculate further on the matter.

WELLS WHICH MOVED

Very often one hears of a well which moved to a new position and the story goes on to give the reason for this. Generally it is said that the well was desecrated when someone washed his hands or washed dirty clothes in the water, or in some other way insulted the well. Many of these stories are mentioned in this book and it is not necessary to mention them again, but one more dramatic than usual may be cited here. It concerns a well called Tobar an t-Solais (Well of Light) which was once in Belgatheran townland in Mellifont parish Co. Louth. It was said that butchers polluted the well by washing the viscera of cattle in it, so the well moved, accompanied by a great number of candles showing light which was seen by all the neighbours.

Often it is said that an enemy caused the holy well to be filled in. This was done at St. Catherine's Well at Killybegs in Co. Donegal, on the instructions of the local rector, and the following day the well bubbled up through the floor of his own house. In my native parish, Outeragh in Co. Leitrim, O'Donovan mentioned a holy well within a few yards of the old parish church, and this is set down on the first Ordnance Survey map of the district. As usual an enemy had the well filled in, so it appeared in the next townland a short distance away, and people now visit the new well on St. Brigid's Day.

The story is told about so many wells that it is necessary to find some natural explanation for it. It may be said that holy wells have been known to dry up following a local drainage scheme. In some cases the well might dry up and as there was no obvious reason for this, some supernatural explanation would be sought. Then it might be said that someone, whom his neighbour did not like, was seen near the well and so the story would get built up. As everyone had heard stories about wells which had been insulted and moved elsewhere, it would be assumed that the well had been insulted also.

The next problem was to find the well in its new position. Anyone who has a thorough knowledge of any part of Ireland and has walked it for one reason or another will have noticed spots that were damp even in a dry summer. There would be no particular difficulty in finding such a spot in many parts of Ireland, and any of these could be recognised as the holy well. In Co. Cork, in Ballydeloughry parish, a story was recorded about a holy well there which was filled in some time before the year 1905. The story continued

'An old man showed me the hollow stump of a sycamore here which is situated on the fence bordering the public road, of the field in which the ruins of Ballybuigh Castle stand. He told me that it held water in the driest summer, even when the neighbouring spring wells ran dry. It was full of water when I saw it at the end of September 1905. The people are inclined to believe that it is the holy well resuscitated, the one which was filled in a long time ago near the old church.'

Two other tree wells are mentioned in the *Ulster Journal of Archaeology*. These are the Pin Well at Coney Island in Co. Armagh and Magherinagaw in Co. Antrim. Both of these are said to have been filled in and in consequence appeared in the hollow stumps of trees.

VI

Healing at Holy Wells and Pilgrimages

For many hundreds of years people have been visiting holy wells and other places associated with the local saint, to pray, and to ask for favours. Many wells and pilgrimages were famous for the cures associated with them, and in some cases people travelled great distances in the hope of a cure. In the *Life of St. Columcille* – written early in the sixteenth century – many healing wells are mentioned and in the middle of the fourteenth century crowds gathered at St. Mullin's to pray and walk in the water of the stream there. 'Some came through devotion, the majority through fear of the plague' as Friar John Clyn recorded at the time.

The practice is of course much older and goes back to the early years of Christianity, and probably some of the wells are even older still. When we come to the eighteenth century the practice can be studied in detail. Smith writing about the pilgrimage to St. Michael's Well at Ballinskelligs in 1756 said:

St. Michael's well near this place is visited every 29th of September by a great concourse of people, some of whom bring their sick blind and lame friends in order as they imagine to be healed by this miraculous water.

At some wells diseases in general were cured but in other cases the well – or the saint – appears to have specialized, and such names as Tobar na Sul – the Eye Well – or Tobar na Plaighe – the Well of the Plague, are typical. Some wells should be visited on special days. The saint's feast day was usually the most popular one, but sometimes there are other days on which the cure may be sought. Sunday is a popular day and Tobar Domhnaigh, – Sunday's Well, – is a familiar name. Still other wells must be visited before sunrise or between sunset and sunrise, or there may be other rules and taboos about the pilgrimage. At some wells, the healing power of the water is greatly increased at special times. Perhaps the most notable of

69

these are the many wells dedicated to St. John the Baptist whose feast day was the 24th June. It was, and is, believed that at midnight between the 23rd and 24th of June the water in the well boiled up, and then, and for the first hour afterwards, 'the water would heal anything'.

In general, the diseases said to be cured are the more obvious ones, those which have been recognised for thousands of years. It must also be said that what are popularly called diseases, are really symptoms each of which may be due to a number of different causes and most of which will clear up quickly no matter what form of treatment may be used. It is therefore impossible to make an exact diagnosis in these cases and so assess the therapeutic power of the well. Such complaints as indigestion, headache or sore eyes may be, and often are, psychogenic in origin, and might be relieved by a visit to a holy well as efficiently as by any other form of psycho-therapy. In addition, it is difficult to imagine any set of circumstances in which a visit to a holy well could do any harm.

People who treat patients will know that the success of any form of treatment is to some extent related to the doctor's enthusiasm for it. At the holy well the sufferer believed in the healing power of the saint, and this belief was shared by nearly all the other pilgrims. This must have had a considerable effect on some patients, and it is easy to see how the reputation of a well could be established by one or two such cures especially if they should occur on the pattern day in the presence of a large crowd. If there was a Life of the local saint available, it would record a list of his more remarkable miracles, and this would be further proof of the saint's power. If, after all this, any further evidence was needed, there were the biblical references to the blind man who was told to 'wash in the pool of Siloe' and the story of the man who waited at the Pool of Bethesda until the water was disturbed. From all this it will be realised that the holy well had many advantages over more physical methods of treatment, whether official or not, and it will also be realised that the holy well was convenient and cheap, while the services of a 'college doctor' were certainly not cheap, even if they were available.

MENTAL ILLNESS

There are some places, and pilgrimages in Ireland which were believed to help patients who suffered from mental illnesses. The best known of these was Gleann na n-Gealt in the parish of Kilgobban in Co. Kerry, which has been mentioned by many writers. Smith mentioned it in 1756, and nearly a hundred years

St. Cravan's Well near Ennistymon, Co. Clare. This well was well known because the water cured diseases of the eyes.

later O'Donovan described it in considerable detail in the *Ordnance Survey Letters*. He wrote of the local belief and went on:

> It is still believed by the natives, that all madmen feel a yearning to make to this valley and that their gloomy disease is relieved by drinking of the clear waters and eating of the water-cresses of Tobar na n-Gealt, the Well of the Lunatics, which is situated in the valley in the North West corner of the townland of Doonore South. They give many instances of mad persons who sojourned in this valley, and returned home, sane and in excellent health, as of a Mary Maher who came into it rabidly mad, and entirely naked in the year 1823 and who returned home (after having spent some months here) sound in mind and stout in health, and of one Sullivan who came into it in the year 1839, and returned entirely cured of his lunacy in three days.

O'Donovan then made reference to a similar practice in ancient Greece where there were three towns each called Anticyra. The people of these places were notable for their custom of growing hellebore which was believed to be a specific for treating mental disorders and the word Anticyra was used as a synonym for bedlam. A similar practice was also mentioned by O'Donovan at Stroov Point in Moville parish Co. Donegal. He learned that a stream gushing from the rock invited 'all the mad and delirious people of the country to drink of its waters'.

In his letters from Co. Louth, O'Donovan described a strange practice in Dunany (Dun Ana) parish. On the seashore there, a stone called Cathaoir Ana (Ana's Chair) was also known as 'the Madman's Chair'. It was believed that insane people from every part of Ireland instinctively went and sat in the chair. Those who did this continued from that time on to the end of their lives with the same degree of sanity or insanity which they had when they sat in the chair. Those people who were responsible for the care of patients took measures to prevent them from sitting in the chair at a time when they were severely disturbed or delirious. Probably the patients were made to sit in the chair during a remission of their symptoms in the hope that the remission would continue indefinitely. If the patient did not get a remission, this could be explained by saying that he had unfortunately sat in Cathaoir Ana so no further improvement was to be expected. In this case Ana was said to have been a female fairy and it is probable that she was the goddess Áine worshipped by the prechristian Irish. I have learned that mad dogs who sat in Cathaoir Ana were also relieved.

The most satisfactory description of one of these places comes from Kilbarry Co. Roscommon. Among a cluster of ancient ruins in the old cemetery there, one is called the *Teach Dorcha* (Dark House). At present the walls are reduced to within a few feet of the ground but O'Donovan found the walls almost complete, and as it contained no windows he suggested that it may have been a penitentiary. The belief was that St. Barry was buried in the doorway of the *Teach Dorcha* and the clay from his grave was especially valuable in curing bellyaches, headaches and other maladies.

When O'Donovan examined the little building he found a pile of straw on the floor as though to make a bed for pigs. It was the practice to take disturbed people to the *Teach Dorcha* on three successive nights of Thursday, Friday and Saturday, and have them sleep on the straw which was spread for them. The ritual was completed when the patients attended Mass in Kilbarry church on Sunday morning. If a patient managed to sleep on all three nights the outlook was thought to be good: if not, it was less satisfactory but here there was a saving clause. It was agreed that to spend the night in the *teach dorcha* would help the patients even though they did not manage to sleep.

This practice, combining diagnosis and treatment is of considerable interest. It is quite likely that many patients suffering from anxiety neuroses, and other such conditions, would benefit from a visit to the *teach dorcha*. A psychotic patient however would not benefit but then it is very unlikely that a psychotic patient would go to such a place, and if he could be persuaded to go he would certainly not sleep there, so the distinction was clearly seen. Probably this method of treatment was worked out by a psychologist of genius who never heard of psychology or of the science of psychiatry.

Sleeping in holy places is reported from different parts of Ireland. On Caher Island, off the coast of Co. Mayo there is a stone called *Leabaidh Phadruig*. It was believed that if an epileptic patient ever slept on it, or even in any part of the holy island his disease would be cured. Patients were also taken to another stone called the *Leacht Mhor* on Cruit Island off Co. Donegal with the intention that they should sleep there, and so have their illnesses cured. Pilgrims also used to sleep near the holy well on Ard Oilean near Slyne Head in Co. Galway.

There have been reports of other methods of treating mental illnesses, notably from Loch Maree in Scotland. In this case one report said that the patient was dipped three times in Loch Maree and another report said that he was towed round the island behind a boat. In 1926 Professor Seamus O'Duilearga heard an account of a similar form of shock therapy from a Co. Kerry shanachy. Unfortunately the treatment was found to be ineffective and was given up but the shanachy said that it had been carried out in his father's time.

Shaw-Mason printed a very good description of the parish of Kilmactige Co. Sligo. In it the writer referred to what he called the use of Lour Oens, i.e. *Leabhar Eoin* (St. John's Gospel). This consisted of:

> the first verse of the Gospel of St. John written on a bit of paper and sewed up in a small piece of cloth, sanctified by a priest's benediction and hung about the person's neck. This they believe will preserve them from the complaint (epilepsy) and also protect them from the power of demons and witches which they believe to have still . . . the power of afflicting the human race with convulsions madness and similar maladies.

SICK CHILDREN

As long as parents continue to care for their children, mothers, and sometimes fathers, will worry about their children's health. The over-anxious mother is well known to doctors, and not rarely, normal healthy children are taken to a succession of doctors, in an effort to allay the anxiety of their parents. Sometimes a child who weighs a pound or two less than 'the baby in the book', is fed with gallons of iron tonics, vitamins, and other placebos in the belief that he is 'delicate.' Similarly parents will bring their children to holy wells, and when the child grows up healthy and strong the saint, or the well, is likely to get the credit for the result.

These holy wells whose virtue is to cure sick children are found in all parts of the country and as a rule they may be visited at any time. Illnesses, real or imaginary, in children, are always urgent. St. Mullin's in Co. Carlow is a notable place of pilgrimage. On the pattern day people took their children there and placed their heads under a spout of water in the belief that this would protect them against some diseases, and this ritual washing during which the children are dipped or sprinkled is used at many of these wells. Among them was Tobar an Ratha Bhain in Aghinagh parish Co. Cork. One of the Ordnance Survey name books says that the water of this well would 'speedily kill or cure infirm children'. In less dramatic language the writer meant that if a delicate infant was taken to the well and immersed in the water before the rising of the sun, it would be seen if the infant's body turned red or pale. It was believed that if the infant turned red it would live but if it turned pale it would die.

In Co. Armagh, at Maghernakely, there was a group of four healing wells. In one of these 'backward children were washed'. There has been a similar practice recorded of a well called Tobar Cranavan in Barragh parish Co. Carlow. Delicate children were taken to the well and bathed in the granite trough which was near the well. In Co. Clare there was a well called Tobar na Taise in Kilnamona parish. The well is in the shape of a coffin and children were placed supine in it, in the hope that they would be restored to health. Still another well in which children were dipped was Tobar Ros (or Tobar Os) in Fahy parish Co. Galway.

Early in the nineteenth century a hostile witness wrote a description of the pilgrimage to Devinish Island, Co. Fermanagh. In it he mentioned the holy well dedicated to St. Molaisse.

In it people with sore eyes, and back going children wash for a cure making what they call a station (a thing I know nothing about) and tye a rag on the thorn according to custom.

In Culdaff parish in Inishowen Co. Donegal is St. Ultan's Well, which is not really a well but a deep pool in a stream just below a waterfall. Delicate children were taken to the 'well' by their mothers who do the station on their behalf. There is now no special day for the pilgrimage but formerly it was done on the first Monday of each quarter. The routine consists of prayers as the pilgrim crosses the stream and goes around an ancient cross and ends as she kneels at the well and recites the Creed. Then, three times, water is taken from the pool and thrown against the cataract. More water is then collected and taken home. Morris in describing this pilgrimage said that formerly there were many rags to be seen tied on the bushes near the well. It will be remembered that the patron saint, Ultan, was a native of Ardbraccan in Co. Meath and during his life he was famous for his care of children.

Some wells are said to cure a common childhood illness – whooping cough. One of these is Tobar Breedia in Darragh parish Co. Limerick. The patient is usually taken to the well to drink the water on the first of February, the feast of St. Brigid, but it may be visited on any day, if one wishes to do so. As part of the treatment, moss which grows near the well is gathered and boiled in milk which the patient should drink. At St. Brigid's Well at Ardagh Co. Longford the moss from around the well is also used if the well is found to be dry.

In Dublin there are a number of holy wells which also cured whooping cough. These included Gregan's Well at Garristown and St. Mochuda's Well, on the edge of the sea at Bunnow. The best known of this group is another seashore well called the Chink Well (Chincough Well) in a cave near Portrane. People seeking a cure leave all sorts of votive offerings at it, so that they may be swept out to sea on the next ebb tide, and if this is seen to occur a favourable result is expected. It is also necessary that this well be visited before sunrise. At St. Duran's Well in Doora parish Co. Clare it was the custom to dip children. This was done in the hope that they would be protected against measles or smallpox or, if the child should contract one of these diseases the attack would be a mild one.

In Kilmeena parish in Co. Mayo St. Brendan's Well is surrounded by a stone wall about three feet high. Inside the wall the floor is paved with stones with the well in a circle about two feet in diameter, in the centre. The well contained about two and a half feet of water, at the end of a long period of dry weather. This well had a most unusual power: it could change the sex of babies if they were dipped in it. It is believed that once the English ordered the destruction of the O'Malley Clan and killed all the male children and babies. However, a baby girl was taken secretly to the well; which was guarded, and dipped, and so turned into a boy, and from him all the O'Malleys are descended.

EYE DISEASES

If we are to judge by the number and popularity of the eye wells, chronic inflammation of the eyes and eyelids must have been common complaints, in Ireland. One reason for this may have been that a great number of the people lived in smoke filled cabins. Other possible causes may have been motes in the eyes, and infections of the roots of the eyelashes. As few people wore spectacles at the time, myopia must have been a severe handicap to many people, and this might be another reason for visiting the holy well. It will also be remembered that some patients come to the doctor complaining of such things as 'spots before the eyes', and there is no doubt that many of these patients would benefit from a visit to a holy well.

As usual there are legends to explain why the well has such healing powers. Some of these legends relate to St. Brigid who was reported to have plucked out her eyes as a method of getting rid of an over enthusiastic and persistent suitor, and then had her sight restored by bathing the wound in the water of the well. One of these wells dedicated to St. Brigid is in Killinagh parish Co. Cavan. In this càse the suitor was Lynagh and when Brigid asked him which of her features he most admired he said he loved her eyes. 'Here they are for you' said Brigid as she plucked them out and threw them on the ground at his feet. She then went to the well, bathed the empty sockets and had her sight restored (O.S. Cavan p. 19). With such a story to back it up, it is no wonder that the well was famous for its power of curing eye diseases. Similar stories about St. Brigid come from Co. Louth but some other female saints are also credited with this dramatic miracle. One of these was St. Caelainn of Kilkeerin parish Co. Roscommon who pulled up a clump of rushes, so causing the healing well to appear.

Only a few of the eye wells may be mentioned. One of these, Tobar na Sool five miles from Ballymena, Co. Antrim, was famous for its power of curing eye diseases until a blind horse was taken and treated there. Following the insult the healing power of the well departed from it. The same story was told about Our Lady's Well in Rochestown parish Co. Limerick. The well was very popular until the blind horse was treated, and then to the surprise of everyone the horse had its sight restored and the owner of the horse was blinded. This is one of the wells which should be visited before sunrise.

Another story of the dangerous power of an eye well is recorded by O'Hanlon. The well, in Boherboy parish Co. Cork, was visited by such large crowds of people that the owner of the land tried to stop them from crossing his field, and arranged to have the well drained. At first his men refused to interfere with the well but finally they were persuaded to begin the work. At the end of the first day they all complained of sore eyes but despite this the work continued for a few more days, as their eyes got steadily worse until all the men went blind. The 'enemy' then decided that the damage must be repaired, the well was reopened and a wall was built round it.

On the top of Slieve Sneacht in Inishowen, Co. Donegal, there is another eye well called as usual Tobar na Sul. The local people had great faith in the power of this well but pilgrims must take care that its water be not muddied or disturbed because this may cause rain and mist to fall on the mountain and make the descent difficult and dangerous.

At some of the eye wells it was customary to leave the piece of cloth which had been used to bathe the sore eyes. This was done at what is called the Rag Well at Diswellstown, Castleknock, Co. Dublin, until Dublin County Council covered the well and put a pump over it, but at present this is no longer used and the healing water is not available. Sunday's Well in Clonmeen parish Co. Cork should be visited on three successive days, Friday, Saturday and Sunday by patients suffering from sore eyes. The story is of a stone mason whose blindness was cured following a visit to the well, and as a grateful patient he carried out the elaborate stonework at the well. There is a similar story about Father O'Donnell's Well on the cliff above the strand at Ardmore, Co. Waterford. Father O'Donnell blessed the well and left in it the power to cure eye diseases, and later, a man called O'Rahilly who was cured there of an eye complaint, built the pillar at the well in gratitude.

HEADACHE

Headache is a common symptom which may have any one of a large number of causes and in a significant number of cases no physical cause can be found for the complaint. It could therefore be expected that some of the sufferers would obtain relief by making a pilgrimage to the holy well and this is found to be the case: some wells and pilgrimages are famous for their power to relieve headaches.

Perhaps the most famous of these is found in Aghabulloge parish Co. Cork. The visit was paid to a round piece of quartzite, known as St. Olan's Cap, and this could be found on the top of an *ogham* inscribed pillar stone called St. Olan's Stone. The 'Cappeen Olan' was credited with many wonderful powers, including the ability to return to its original position if removed to any distance however great. To place it on the head and walk three times round the neighbouring church was specific for headache.

The Cappeen became an object of such superstitious practices that the original was made away with by the clergyman of the parish: another however soon made its appearance but much inferior to its predecessor.

In this case, even the denunciation by the parish priest could not completely destroy people's faith in the power of St. Olan's Cap.

At some wells it was the custom to make a visit on three successive days to obtain relief from headache. One of these was at All Saints in Reynagh parish Co. Offaly, where formerly there was a group of seven wells: one of these wells was visited by those seeking relief from any disease of the head but its special success was in relieving headaches. In Athnowen parish in Co. Cork there are two wells quite close together called Mary's Well and Sunday's Well, both of which are visited as part of the pilgrimage. Patients suffering from headache, earache or toothache were believed to benefit especially, and as at All Saints, it is the custom to make the pilgrimage three times. Here there is a difference, because it is necessary to make the three visits either on Friday, Sunday and the following Friday, or on Sunday, Friday and Sunday. This period of eight days would normally be long enough to allow most cases of toothache or earache to clear up, or to show definite improvement and the three visits were likely to benefit many cases of headache.

In Oranmore parish Co. Galway there are two flagstones one of which was believed to bear the imprint of St. Patrick's head and two smaller impressions which were made by his knees. The hollow made by the saint's head measures 16″ × 18″ and is 8″ deep, and a sufferer might obtain relief from her headache by kneeling and placing her head in this hollow.

There is a similar story told of St. Brochan in Clonsast parish in Offaly. Some distance south east of the old ruined church there and across a small brook a stone on which St. Brochan stamped the impression of his head can be found. As at Oranmore people suffering from headaches, visit the stone and place their heads in the hollow and are often relieved.

At many wells the water is believed to cure headaches but a special ritual may be necessary to obtain the cure. One of these was St. Brigid's Well in Kilranelagh parish Co. Carlow. The well is in the old cemetery there and a stream from it runs to a stone trough in an adjacent field, and the water in the stone trough is used to cure headaches. Kilcolman parish in Co. Waterford is said to be the oldest parish in Ireland and has a famous healing well. As part of the station sufferers bathe their heads in the sacred water and drink some of it to be relieved of their headaches and I was assured locally that many sufferers are so relieved by the power of St. Colman.

St. Ciaran's Well at Castlekeeran near Kells Co. Meath is very well known, and many stories can be heard about its powers. A spring well rises on the side of a small hillock and the stream from it flows into a brook which joins the River Blackwater, a short distance away. On its way to the brook the tiny stream forms three smaller wells one of which is known to cure headaches. This is one of the many wells of which the healing power of the water is greatly increased at certain times. In this case the special day is the first Sunday in August and people still visit the well at midnight when the water boils up.

Two more examples of practices which relieved headaches may be given. Near the ruined cathedral at Clonmacnoise there is a hollow stone which usually contains some water. Having completed the station the sufferer places her head in the hollow and then blesses herself with the water. Again I have been assured that many

79

sufferers have been relieved following this practice. The other example comes from the Curragh of Kildare when pilgrims do stations at Father Moore's Well. Having completed the station, pilgrims, who wished to have their headaches relieved, went to a house near the well where the hat of Father Moore [1779–1826] was kept.

The sufferer after visiting the well . . . and reciting some prayers, places the hat on the head and obtains relief.

It is clear that the success of these rituals at special times and places, is mainly due to the excellent psychotherapy involved. There has always been a need for such psychotherapy, and at all times physicians have used it, whether they realised it or not, but only during the last century official medicine has become aware of this need. Since the medicine of the eighteenth and nineteenth century was not generally aware of this need, it was good that the holy well was able to help some of the cases. It may have been that Father Moore was a psychologist of genius, whose success at the time could only be thought to be supernatural.

BACKACHE

Backache is also a common symptom and sometimes a disabling one. In many cases the patient has little physical evidence to back up her, or his, complaints and generally the sufferers get little sympathy from their friends. In such cases it would be expected that some holy wells would relieve the pain and this is found to be the case. On the strand at Ardmore Co. Waterford there is a large flagstone on which St. Declan is said to have travelled to Ireland, and on St. Declan's Day, 24th July, it is still the custom to crawl under this stone as a method of relieving backache. One nineteenth century writer, Philip Dixon-Hardy, described this practice of crawling under the stone, and was horrified – so he said – at the sight of the girls' legs, generously displayed in the process. This most unladylike leg show was probably enjoyed by everybody present, including the girls themselves, especially by those who were blessed with shapely legs, and no doubt they benefited by the exercise. As usual there was a difficulty. The treatment would not be successful if the patient while performing the exercise had on his or her person anything which had been borrowed or stolen.

The same practice is carried out at Kilronan Co. Roscommon. There the flagstone is called St. Ronan's Mass Table and is raised about two feet above ground level on four stone supports. The exercise is not as easy as it appears and I was told by a big man who had done it, an experienced miner, that some of the efforts made by men to crawl under the stone were a source of amusement for the bystanders. He did not think that the sight of the girls' legs was unladylike.

At Devinish Island Co. Fermanagh there is a different ritual for the treatment of backache. Early in the nineteenth century a certain 'J. Frith, Philomath' a hostile witness wrote an interesting description of Devinish. As part of this he wrote:

> Ten yards northward [from the house of St. Molaise] is St. Mullushe's bed which is only a stone trough sunk in the ground, 6 feet long and 15 inches wide at the shoulders. It has a very uneven bottom composed of three rough stones. In it people afflicted with a pain in their backs lie down for a cure and say several Ave Marias and other prayers around the same.

The writer goes on:

> Both Mulashe's bed and well have of late years lost their repute (even in my time) and are very little frequented as the most ignorant found out that they were not infallible in curing the complaints of everyone who had belief in them and at any rate Superstition and Idolatry are every day wearing away more and more.

I understand that pilgrims still visit Devinish.

Two other practices used for the relief of backache may be mentioned. At Clonmacnoise there is a large stone in the ancient cemetery there, on which the sufferers sit to have their pains relieved. There is another such stone near St. Columcille's Well at Gleneaney in Inver parish Co. Donegal. This stone, situated in the cemetery, is concave and the patients press their backs into the concavity.

On the top of Mount Brandon there is a pillar stone called Leac na nDrom (the Stone of the Backs). Pilgrims who sought a cure for backache stood with their backs against this stone. It is not likely that anyone whose backache was due to physical disease would undertake the climb to the top of Mount Brandon.

OBSTETRICS AND GYNAECOLOGY

There are many wells at which pilgrims sometimes pray for children. One of these is a well on the top of a hill called Knockroe, near the ruins of the Cistercian Abbey of Knockmoy, Co. Galway. The well, now dedicated to St. Bernard, was the site of a famous pilgrimage on 20th August, the feast of St. Bernard but according to Maire Mac Neill the pilgrimage is much older, and may be a prechristian festival.

Another famous pilgrimage was to St. Brigid's Well, in the village of Brideswell in Co. Roscommon and the most popular day was the last Sunday of July. Weld visited the village in 1832 and wrote a description of what he found:

> the old building on the far side of the village green next to the well . . . Over the doorway leading into the bath enclosure appears a coat of arms, neatly carved in stone and in tolerable preservation with the following inscription 'built by the Right Honourable Sir Randall MacDonnell first Earl of Antrim, 1625.'

The story is that MacDonnell and his wife, a daughter of Red Hugh O'Neil, were childless and made the pilgrimage to Tobar Bhride to pray for children. Following the pilgrimage, a son and heir was born to them and in gratitude the earl built the gateway to the bath-house in 1625.

It is quite likely that people prayed for children at many holy wells but did not speak openly about it. Recently I learned of a statue to Our Lady, which was put on a tree near Tobar Mhuire near Shankill Cross in Co. Roscommon. This was done some years ago by a man who had visited the well and prayed for children, and put up the statue in gratitude to Our Lady when his prayer had been answered.

At the pilgrimage to Cruach Patrick, one of the stations is called St. Patrick's Bed. At present this is visited by all the pilgrims but Dixon Hardy quoting from a book by the Rev. James Page said that in his time, the early nineteenth century, this station was visited only by those who desired children. These pilgrims stayed all night on the mountain and slept in St. Patrick's Bed.

At Tobar Eidhne on Inishmore in Galway Bay women prayed for children while men prayed at another well a short distance away.

There are some practices which are believed to ensure the safe delivery of children. One of these was concerned with the piece of quartzite called St. Olan's Cap which has been mentioned as having the power to cure headaches. The stone was also believed to help 'certain female complaints and was frequently borrowed as a talisman for women in travail.' Another wonder-working stone was mentioned in Beatha Coluimb Chille. This was the stone known as St. Columcille's Pillow which was then preserved on Tory Island and 'works many miracles and marvels, and water wherein it is steeped doth succour women in labour forthwith, how little so ever they may drink thereof.' St. Columcille's clay from Gartan Co. Donegal is also said to have many wonderful powers 'and every woman in pangs of childbirth that eateth thereof is helped forthwith.'

In Lough Gill Co. Sligo there is an island called Inishmore where there are the ruins of an ancient church believed to have been founded by St. Loman.

> In a rock near the door of the church is a cavity called Our Lady's Bed which is said to be favourable to women in pregnancy who fondly imagine that by going into it, and turning thrice round saying at the same time some prayers they shall not die in labour.

Wilde described a similar practice from Glendalough Co. Wicklow. He found that 'ladies often climbed up to St. Kevin's Bed there in the belief that by lying in the bed they would not die in childbirth.'

On Inishmurray off the Coast of Co. Sligo there was a very

One of the praying "altars" on Inishmurray, a holy island off the coast of Co. Sligo. See also pp. 141—3.

ancient practice intended to ensure a safe delivery. Inside the ancient cashel there are the ruins of a church called Teampull na bFear and near it there is a pillar stone facing east and west, with an ancient cross incised on the west face. Near each side of the west face there is a hole large enough to hold a thumb and on the two lateral sides the holes are large enough to take the fingers. Women nearing confinement kneel at the stone and pray for a successful delivery. They then place their thumbs in the holes in the east face and grasp the stone with their fingers in the side openings, and by this means raise themselves from their knees.

This is said to ensure a safe delivery and 'the natives of the island assert as proof of its efficacy that death resulting from childbirth is unknown amongst them.'

There are some ways in which it is possible to get the power to help women in labour. O'Donovan found that a wooden statue of St. Brendan was preserved on Inis Gluaire off the coast of Co. Mayo and it was said that if you were to take this statue in your hands three times in the name of the Three Persons of the Blessed Trinity you would receive the power to help a woman in labour by touching her with your hands. Another method of acquiring this power is that the individual should span the shaft of the High Cross of Clonmacnoise. I was assured by a man who had spanned the cross, and was known to have done so, that he had been asked to help women in labour, and had done it successfully by putting his arm around the patient. Most of his skill is now used in veterinary obstetrics.

TOOTHACHE

St. Brigid's Well at Greaghnafarna townland in Co. Leitrim is one of the toothache wells. A pilgrim suffering from toothache must go to the well and say five Paters, five Aves and a Creed. He then must make a promise to the saint that he will not shave or polish shoes on Sunday, and then he blesses himself with the water, and applies some of it to the painful tooth. Finally he must add a stone to the cairn beside the well, and leave a stone, a pin or a coin at the well. If the promise not to shave or polish shoes is broken, the toothache will return.

Among the other wells whose virtue is to cure toothache there is one on Carnsore Point, Co. Wexford, which is dedicated to a certain St. Boec. Two wells which have already been mentioned, Mary's Well and Sunday's Well, in Athnowen parish Co. Cork are also visited by people seeking relief from toothache. During this pilgrimage a decade of the rosary is recited at each of nine stations as the pilgrim moves clockwise around both wells. It is also necessary that the wells be visited three times over a period of eight days.

There is a Co. Donegal well called Tobar Bride which is a famous healing well. The older name was Tobar Aibheog, which was the name of a Celtic goddess, and there are clear references to pre-christian beliefs connected with it. It was firmly believed that:

> If you leave a medal or beads or even a little white stone at it, and drink some of the water it would cure the toothache or anything of that kind . . . Anyone with toothache who went and made the station and took three sips of the water the toothache died away.

Some unusual stories are told about this well. The supernatural cow, the Glas Gaibhleann, appeared at it and gave a quart of milk to everyone until people began to quarrel about who should own her, so she went away 'and nobody saw her go'. The water will not boil and Morris heard a story of a tooth abscess which burst when bathed with the healing water.

Three Co. Dublin Holy wells were said to cure toothache. One of these was St. Movee's Well at Grange which also cured headache and sore throat. Another was St. Senan's Well at Slade and the third was St. Catherine's Well at Drumcondra. This was in a townland called Drisoge, which was on the north bank of the river Tolka, and in 1928 was under a kitchen floor. In spite of this it was an important well because the water cured toothache, sore eyes, and chincough.

Two other toothache wells were St. Fiachra's Well at Ullard, Graiguenamanagh, and St. Columcille's Well at Sandyford, Co. Carlow. The water of St. Fiachra's Well also cured rheumatic pains, as well as toothache, and in addition it preserved people from shipwreck. St. Columcille's Well not only relieved toothache, it also cured sores, hoarseness and some other diseases.

In Outeragh parish in Co. Leitrim the pilgrimage to the holy well might be done by those seeking relief from toothache, and this might be done by proxy, and I have heard of pay being offered to the substitute. In a hole in a wall of the old ruined church at Kilbarry, Co. Roscommon a skull is still preserved: I saw it there recently. Sufferers from toothache take the skull, and apply it to the tender area which is rubbed gently with the skull, and I was assured that it is still used successfully.

In some cases these treatments could be helpful. We all have heard of the patient whose painful tooth got better as soon as he went to the dentist, and a visit to a holy well might have the same effect. This and other conservative methods such as the application of a skull to the tender area could do little harm at a time when the usual efforts to extract a tooth were always painful, and might be disastrous.

SPRAINS, WOUNDS AND RHEUMATISM

Sprains and such injuries are sometimes treated by tying a string with nine knots around the injured part and repeating the words of a narrative charm. Crawford described one such practice from the Sligo Leitrim border. The story was that St. Patrick was not allowed to cross the river Garvogue by the ford at Sligo so he rode around Lough Gill through very rough country where his horse injured the tendons of his foot. The saint then used a number of stones to cure his horse, and left the cure on the stones. These stones, seven of them, can be found on a rough horizontal slab, in an old graveyard two miles west of Drumahaire. The stones are rounded, and vary from six inches, up to eleven inches in diameter. Nearby is a small peg-like stone placed upright in the ground. When needed people apply the stones to the site of injury, and in case of strained tendons a piece of thread found tied around the peg stone is used. This piece of thread is taken home and tied around the site of the injury, and is replaced by another piece of thread to be used by the next patient.

There is a less elaborate ritual at St. Declan's Well at Ardmore, Co. Waterford. The sufferer visits the well and bathes the injured limb in the water. Tobar Mhuire near Elphin, Co. Roscommon, is well known for its healing powers. I was told recently of its power by a man living near the well who suffered a severe injury to his foot. He sat by the well for some hours, while he bathed the injured foot with the water, and at the end of the time was surprised to find that the foot was still very painful. He hobbled home to bed, and in the morning his foot had completely recovered and his faith in the power of the well was confirmed.

In Kilteevan parish Co. Roscommon there was a holy well called Tobar na Greaghta (Well of the Injuries) which was believed to cure all sorts of wounds and sores. Unhappily an enemy (Robert Ormsby) washed the broken leg of a greyhound in the water, and at this insult the well disappeared underground.

O'Donovan described a holy 'well' called Eas Damhnata in Lavey parish Co. Cavan. Near this was a large stone resembling a millstone, in which there was a cavity large enough to hold two or three quarts of water. Those who do the station, bathe their knees in the water in the cavity and as a result all their wounds are healed.

St. Fiachra's Well at Ullard already mentioned has some peculiar powers. The water is used to treat rheumatic pains as well as other pains. Near the well are two stones. One bears the imprint of St. Fiachra's knees, and the other is part of an old quern stone. Water from the well is first placed in the hollows in both stones and is then used to treat sores on the body.

Rheumatic complaints are relieved by the water of a well called Tobar Finnain, on Valentia Island, Co. Kerry, and also by the water of Tobar an Ratha Bhain in Aghinagh parish Co. Cork. At Mullinakill in Rosbercon parish, Co. Kilkenny, there is a well dedicated to St. Moling. Here the saint is said to have used the water to cure the ulcers from which he suffered and it has been so used ever since.

Near Tobar na nAingeal in Co. Donegal, there are seven rounded stones which give relief if they are applied to sores and seats of physical pain and the water of Lady Well at Tyrellstown, Co. Dublin, was used to treat sprains, bruises and rheumatism.

In Rathkeale parish Co. Limerick the water of St. Bernard's Well cured many diseases including rheumatism, lameness and sore eyes. Also in Co. Limerick, the saint's well in Ardpatrick parish cured rheumatism, lameness and rickets. In the same parish Danaher recorded the story of the pilgrim who was unable to see his reflection in the well. This was known to be a very bad omen and to confirm this, the pilgrim died within a year.

This group of diseases, sprains, wounds and rheumatism is a very vague one. There must have been many very simple conditions which cleared up quickly, and such cases would establish the reputation of the well. In any case the number and variety of treatments used for rheumatism is almost infinite, so perhaps the water of a holy well might find a place among them.

MISCELLANEOUS HEALING

Some holy wells were said to cure diseases of the stomach and bowels. One of these was Tobar a Tresnane, three miles north of Ardmore, Co. Waterford and another was The Blessed Well in Ballingarry parish Co. Limerick. In this case it was necessary that the well be visited and the water drunk before breakfast.

At St. Finnian's church at Killemlagh, Co. Kerry, pilgrims go seeking the cure of 'diseases of a scrofulous nature' on 16th March. The story is that St. Finnian was a leper and used a fern which grew on the walls of the ruined church there to treat this leprosy, and in this way the herb was given its healing power. The fern is called *cos dubh* (black foot) and has been identified as *Asplenium Adiantum*

Nigrum which is also used to treat other skin diseases.

At some wells a visit might preserve the pilgrim from all diseases for the coming year. One such well on Valentia Island is dedicated to St. Finan and was visited on 17th March. A pilgrimage to St. Sgreabhan's Well and to his Bed in Clondagad parish. Co. Clare might be made by people suffering from sore eyes. This 'well' is a waterfall twenty feet high and the 'bed' is a recess in the face of a cliff near the well. In addition to having their sore eyes cured, people who visit this well are protected against the fairies.

Another notable well is Tobar Halamog in Salterstown parish Co. Louth. The patron day was 7th June and the well cured agues and other afflictions. On Dalkey Island, in Dublin Bay, there are the ruins of an old church, and a holy well, both dedicated to the local saint, Begnet. The water of the well was said to cure scurvy. A legend recorded in the Life of St. Columcille explains why a holy well on the east side of Lough Foyle was called Tobar na Deilg (Well of the Thorn). It says that when the saint suffered from a thorn in his foot, he treated it by bathing the wound in the water, and consequently the healing power remained in the water.

There are a number of references to special areas within which the power of the saint protected people against certain diseases. In the *Life of Columcille* it is said that during a epidemic of the Buidhe Chonnail (Yellow Plague) the saint fled to Tir Connail and when he came to the river Bir the plague did not cross it and 'has not done it to this day'. The river has been identified as the River Moyola in Co. Derry.

O'Donovan mentioned an old ruined church on a point of land in Lough Owel, Co. Westmeath. The church is called Teampull Phort Lomain and was the site of a famous pilgrimage. It was said that at a time when plague was spreading all through Ireland, St. Loman prayed and it never entered the area of his jurisdiction. As proof of this story I learned that during the great 'flu epidemic of 1918 it never spread to St. Loman's district.

Near Killeaden, Co. Mayo, there are three stones each of which contains a *bullaun* (hollow). One of these stones is east of the road from Balla to Kiltimagh. The second stone is a little to the east of Ballinamore House and the third stone is between Ballinamore and Kiltimagh. The story is that St. Patrick knelt on each stone to pray, leaving in each case the impression of his knee, i.e. the *bullaun*. It was also believed that within the triangular area formed by the three stones everyone was safe from destruction and war.

VII

Trees at Holy Wells

Praying at special trees and walking around them is part of the pilgrimage ritual at many Irish holy wells. Sacred and special trees have always been important in the social and religious life of the Irish and in our oldest records there are references to these special trees. It is very likely that this tree worship takes us back to the beginning of the Irish as a people and to a religion that is much older than Christianity. Here it is not necessary, or even wise, to try to peer into this land of twilight where the imagination might assume greater importance than the facts. In *The Holy Wells of Wales* Francis Jones wrote:

> Wells associated with trees are not numerous in Wales but some 30 examples have been noted and there are probably more. But the traditions and ritual concerning them are so much in sympathy with the tree-well association in other Celtic lands, as well as in Celtic antiquity that it is difficult not to recognise in them a ragged remnant of what was formerly a widespread custom.

In their book, *The Celtic Realms*, Dillon and Chadwick mention the Gaulish druids 'who dwell in deep groves and sequestered uninhabited woods.' They also mention a sacred wood near Marseilles which was felled by Caesar and 'the superstitious dread of the natives who were called upon to cut down the trees.' In Britain the word *nemet* meant a sacred grove and on Anglesea, 'The religious groves dedicated to superstition and barbarous sites were levelled to the ground' by the invading Romans. These references, and there are many others, show that trees were honoured as part of the ancient Celtic religion and in Ireland this has continued until the present day.

HISTORY

Whatever may be said about these early references, it is possible to use early Irish records to learn a little about what our less remote ancestors thought about these special trees. Sacred trees are mentioned in Irish records since the tenth century. In the Irish Language the word for such a tree was *bilé* and this word is found in many Irish place-names. Examples are Moville (Magh a' bhile) in Co. Donegal and Tobar a' bhile in Kilcrohane parish in Co. Kerry. Others are Aghavilla in Co. Leitrim, Cornavilla in Co. Cavan and Rathvilly in Co. Carlow, and many more might be cited. The word *bilé* is not used in modern Irish.

In 980 the *Chronicum Scotorum* says: 'Dal Cais was plundered by Maelsechlainn son of Domhnall and the *bilé* of Magh-Adhair was cut down.' This place is now called Moyre, near Tullach in Co.Clare, and it was under this tree that the O'Brien lords of the Dal Cais were inaugurated. Nearly seventy years later, in 1049, we get: 'The tree of Magh-Adhair was thrown down by Aedh O'Connor.' The O'Briens got some revenge in 1089 when Murchertach O'Brien raided into Connacht 'and he felled the Ruadhbetech'. This was the inaugural tree of the O'Connors at Roevehagh Co. Galway, and the name, Ruadhbetheach, (Red beech), would indicate that the tree was a copper beech. As these trees were believed to be immortal it must have been possible to renew them.

Similar inter-tribal rivalry in Ulster resulted in the destruction of more sacred trees. In 1099 the *Annals of Ulster* say: 'Thereafter the Ulaidh abandon the camp and the Cinel-Eogain burn it and cut down the Craebh-telcha,' i.e. the sacred tree of the people of East Ulster. As could be expected the Ulaidh took revenge and in the year 1111 'The Ulaidh (went) on a hosting into Cinel Eogain and cut down the trees of Tulach Oc,' where the O'Neil lords were inaugurated.

In the *Lives of the Irish Saints* there are references to these special trees. Even though the *Lives* are not now regarded as historical documents they reflect the opinions of the time in which they were written, – the 11th – 12th centuries. There are references to St. Kevin's yew tree at Glendalough and Geraldus Cambrensis recorded a story about St. Kevin's willow tree which bore apples to cure a sick boy. He also told a story of a group of archers who cut down the saint's trees at Finglas:

But they were forthwith smitten by God whose divine indignation reserves vengeance to himself and condescends to vindicate the injuries offered to his saints on earth by a sudden and singular pestilence: so that most of them miserably perished within a very few days.

There is another early reference to St. Brigid's Oak near her great church at Kildare. It reads:

For there was a very high oak tree there which St. Brigid loved much and blessed: of which the trunk still (C. AD 980) remains: no one dares to cut it with a weapon but he who can break off any part of it with his hands deems it a great advantage, hoping for the aid of God by means of it, because through the miracles of St. Brigid, many miracles have been performed by that wood.

The *Annals of Ulster* in 1056 say 'Lightning came and killed three persons at Disert-Tola and a student at Sord and broke down the *bilé.*'

This reverence for special trees continued into later centuries. In the *Life of St. Columcille* written early in the sixteenth century there is a story of the saint's oak tree at Kells. When it fell some of the bark was taken and used to tan leather, which was then used to make a pair of boots. The wearer of the boots got leprosy. Also in the sixteenth century a lament for a *bilé* was written by Laoiseach mac an Bhaird. There is nothing in the poem to indicate where the tree grew but it was a thorn tree, and it appears that it was destroyed by an enemy. This is Bergin's translation of one stanza:

'It has been cut away our bitter ruin:
The comely thorn that was a store house for the bird:
A thorn like it never grew from the soil:
To me until death it will be a cause of tears.'

ORIGIN OF THE TREES

Generally the trees were believed to be due to a miracle of the local saint. An example of this is St. Colman's sacred tree in 'the old parish' three miles north of Ardmore, Co. Waterford. The story is that as St. Colman was walking near his old church he stuck a little dry stick in the ground. The stick took root and grew into a tree which never can be destroyed. This story is told about many sacred trees. One of these was a great old ash tree which grew over St. Patrick's Well in Kilcorkey parish in Co. Roscommon. The tree was called St. Patrick's Walking-stick. Also, in Listerling parish Co. Kilkenny, there was an old thorn tree over the holy well there which was said to have grown from St. Moling's walking-stick.

A striking version of this story was recorded by Otta Swire from the Isle of Skye in the Hebrides. It tells of a priest from the island of Pabay, shortly after the time of St. Columcille, who was on a journey through the forest to visit some of his flock. Once while he sat down to rest he found himself surrounded by a crowd of the Little People who approached him in fear. One of them managed to explain that they had repented of their sins and asked him to forgive them but when he learned who they were he refused to forgive them and sent them away. One old woman pleaded with him and quoted 'there is joy in heaven over one sinner who does penance' and she also quoted in despair 'and him who cometh to me, I will in no wise cast out.' Then they all disappeared.

The priest was disturbed and continued his journey forgetting his stick which he had stuck in the ground and when he looked for it on his return he found that it had grown into a great ash tree. The priest knelt and prayed, and called on the Little People to come back to him, but they never came back and only the helpless wailing answered him. He went off, and lived in the forest, and preached the forgiveness of God to all who would listen. Men said he was mad, and he never saw the Little People again, but gradually the wailing got less and in the end he could no longer hear it.

Another legend tells of the origin of the sacred tree of Clenor, called the Crann a'hulla in Annakissa, two miles south east of Doneraile Co. Cork. In this case a beautiful girl called Craebhnat, refused to marry the son of the king of Munster, and when he came to carry her off, she plucked out one of her eyes and threw it on the ground. From the spot where the eye fell the sacred ash tree grew up. Another sacred tree was known as the Crann Comaita (Tree of Power). This was an ash, and it was believed that St. Patrick met the Prince of Munster under its branches and the prince asked Patrick to have it bear apple blossoms. The saint did so. This is a version of the legend of the tree called the Eo Mugna which was an oak, and yet was able to produce apples and hazel nuts as well as acorns.

It would be easy to quote more legends about the many famous trees like the Cuaille Mic Duach at Kilmacduagh. A modern tree story is told by O'Donovan in the *Ordnance Survey Letters* from Galway. He wrote that in the graveyard at Ballintubber, Co. Mayo, he saw an ash tree growing over the grave of a notorious priest hunter known as Sean na Sagart. The tree was twisted and blasted and was looked upon as an emblem of deformity. During a visit to Ballintubber in 1971 I failed to find this tree or any memory of it.

IMMORTAL TREES

There are many stories told, to illustrate the immortality of the sacred trees. A famous whitethorn grows in a green spot in the middle of the road at Seir Ciaran in Co. Offaly. The tree was originally on the roadside and when the road was being widened the Local Authority deferred to the authority of the saint so the road was diverted, leaving the tree standing in a green spot in the centre. When I visited it in 1974 the tree was a young whitethorn, with the stump of an old one beside it. A local man, Mr. Conway, clearly a good witness, aged about 65, told me that when a young man he noticed that the old tree, with its five arms, was beginning to die. Greatly disturbed by this, because he had always been told that it could not die, he asked the oldest man around – Tom Mulrany. The old man was able to reassure him, he had seen this happen before, and a new one would grow, so he watched as the old one died and a young one grew up beside it.

From Co. Donegal, O'Donovan described a famous holly tree which he saw on 21st October 1835. It was in Glencolumcille and the story was that as St. Columcille approached, a pole thrown by one of the demons, who were resisting the saint, struck and killed one of his companions. Columcille threw the pole back and it stuck in the ground and grew into the tree which O'Donovan saw. Whatever about its truth the story is more than four hundred years old since it was told in Manus O'Donnell's *Life of St. Columcille*.

There are other trees which are said to have renewed themselves. These include the tree at St. Moling's Well at Mullinakill Co. Kilkenny. This is believed to have been planted by the saint and the people say that it has renewed itself many times. The wood of this tree is used as a talisman against fire, and twigs were taken by people who wished to protect their property. Perhaps the best documented 'immortal' tree is the Crann a'hulla, already mentioned, near Doneraile in Co. Cork. It is a stunted ash and is believed to be 300 years old. Another is a large holly tree over a holy well at Ballincrea in Myshall parish Co. Carlow. This one has demonstrated its immortality by growing from the stem of its predecessor.

It would be regarded as a sacrilege to injure or even to insult the saint's tree and many stories are told, and believed, about the punishment which is sure to follow such an act. One such story is told of a man who broke off some twigs from St. Colman's sacred tree near Ardmore, Co. Waterford, and carried them home to burn. As he came in sight of his house, it appeared to be on fire, so he dropped the sticks and ran to put out the fire. When he reached home, there was no fire so he went back and picked up the sticks but again the house appeared to be on fire and again he ran to put it out, but again the fire disappeared. When this happened for the third time he was more determined and continued to carry the sticks until he reached home and found his house burned down. This story is told about the wood of some other sacred trees such as the ash tree at St. Patrick's Well at Kellistown, Co. Carlow, but I have not found any version in which the individual left back the wood and so saved his house. On the ground around the sacred ash tree over St. Patrick's Well, in Kilcorkey parish Co. Roscommon, there were several large branches which had fallen. These were never taken away, even in times when fuel was scarce.

When the ash tree at St. Olan's Well in Aghabulloge parish Co. Cork, was cut down by order of the parish priest, it was found that the wood did not burn and those who did it 'never had a day's luck.' Unfortunately the story does not say what misfortune befell the parish priest. Many of the stories say that the wood of the sacred tree will not burn, but there is never any direct evidence for this belief. Few people would dare to try the experiment and if anyone ever did try it he would never dare to tell his neighbours. Another story of the consequences of burning the wood is told about a tree at St. John's Well, in Kiltegan parish, Co. Carlow. When the tree fell people took some of the wood to burn but it exploded in the fire. It is possible that this story is true even though the explosion may not have been supernatural.

There is a dramatic story about how the saint punished a man who insulted her tree at St. Brigid's Well near Buttevant, Co. Cork. In this case the offender (a Protestant policeman from Co. Galway) was so unwise as to amuse himself by swinging on the branches of the tree. When he got back to the police station at Churchtown he got violent pains in his limbs and died six months later.

There is always another story of the misfortunes which befell those who interfered with the saint's tree. At St. Columcille's Well at Sandyford, Co. Carlow, an enemy (Captain Lawrence) tried to cut down the bush which was growing beside the well. He found that he was unable to do it and as punishment his head was permanently bent towards one side. Previously he had tried to fill in the well but when he had done this and turned to move away, the well was seen to be unaffected.

At Seir Ciarain in Co. Offaly, an enemy (Harding of Grange House) told his workmen to cut off one of the branches of the saint's whitethorn which then overhung the road and caused him some

The sacred thorn tree at Seir Ciaran in Co. Offaly. The tree stands on a green island in the middle of the road. Many votice offerings, rags and rosaries can be seen hanging from the branches. The stump of the old tree is close by.

inconvenience as he drove past. They refused so he rushed off to do it himself. As he struck the first blow with an axe, he was stricken with facial palsy, which badly disfigured him for the rest of his life.

At Abbeylara in Co. Longford, there is a very holy well called Tobar Ri an Domhnaigh. In O'Donovan's time two ancient trees, an ash and a whitethorn, grew over the well. In this story a man was so foolhardy as to cut some branches from them for firewood, but when he brought home the wood he was upbraided by his wife. Shortly afterwards 'he went into a decline and died'.

At Ballinacrea Well in Myshall parish Co. Carlow, a young girl cut some of the bushes which formed a fence around the well; she got a stroke and 'never did any good afterwards'. There is a similar story about a thorn tree at Tober Doney, Halsly's Town in Co. Down. A daughter of the house who was 'queer' chopped down the tree. Later she got so bad that it was necessary to send her to an institution. In Donoughmore parish in Co. Cork, the whitethorns which grew at the original site of St. Laghteen's Well were held very sacred. Once someone took an axe to cut one of them down, but suddenly he got a pain in his belly and was forced to stop. There was a famous tree at Lough Ciarain, in Co. Mayo, on which spancels and halters for cattle were hung. O'Donovan said that it had been cut down on the instructions of the bishop of the diocese. I have not been able to learn if any misfortune followed this, but it is likely that in this case the authority of the bishop would outweigh that of St. Ciaran.

VIII

Stones at Holy Wells

The veneration of stones is often a part of the ritual carried out during pilgrimages to holy wells. The origin of this cult of stones does not concern us here, and whether it is prechristian or even pre-Celtic are questions which may be left to others. What is important here, is that this practice has continued in Ireland, in some cases well into the twentieth century and can still be examined in some detail. In a number of cases it may be the practice to add another stone to a cairn of stones near the well, or the pilgrim may scratch a cross on some special stone. Stones may be arranged in the shape of a 'chair' or of a 'bed,' on which the pilgrim may sit or lie. White stones or other specially coloured ones, may be considered holy or endowed with some other supernatural power. At some places of pilgrimage, small heaps of stones, or single large stones, mark the stations at which pilgrims pray or around which they walk. A monolith may be carved in the shape of a primitive cross or a cross may be incised on a flat surface and the pilgrims may kiss the cross or bow to the stone as part of the ritual. In some cases, the stone may be carved to represent a human face, which is said to be the face of the saint.

Many of the stones were believed to have special powers. These are mentioned by nineteenth century writers who, with a singular lack of understanding, often dismiss them by saying 'the stone was used for superstitious purposes', but rarely give any more information. Some of the stones have had holes made through them. These are often credited with strange powers and have an air of mystery about them, but nobody has ever explained why the holes were made. Still another group of stones are believed to have the power of returning to their proper places, no matter how often or how far they may be removed. Of all these special stones, the most dramatic were those used for swearing or cursing. These were the object of the most violent opposition by the Catholic clergy all

"The Priest Stone", Sceillig Mhichil.

through the nineteenth century and I have not been able to learn that such stones are still being turned, although at least one did survive into this century. The most usual of the special stones are those which bear the imprint of the saint's knee, or hand, or foot, or head, or, in one case, the imprint of his bottom.

A much quoted reference from St. Adamnan's *Life of St. Columcille* may be the source of some of these practices. It reads:

> In the same district mentioned above, he (St. Columcille) took a white stone from the river (Ness) and blessed it so that it should

98

effect some cures. Contrary to nature that stone when imersed in water floated like an apple. This divine miracle was performed in the presence of King Brude and his household.

This story may have given rise to some of the belief in the healing powers of white stones. Floating stones are often found in stories of Irish saints, even though one may wonder if St. Columcille had found a piece of pumice.

HEAPS OF STONES

These are, or were, to be seen on the roadsides in some parts of Ireland, as well as being found near holy wells and such places. By the roadside, they often marked the place where some notable event occurred, but these reasons are now being forgotten. In one case, on some roads leading to the ancient cemetery at Clonmacnoise, heaps of stones marked the places where the bearers placed the coffin to rest. In his book on Lough Corrib, Wilde wrote of the roads leading to St. Mary's Abbey at Cong:

> So on all sides we meet with wayside monuments, crosses, pillar-stones and tumuli erected by those who composed the passing funerals, as they rested at any of these spots on their way to the hallowed precincts of St. Mary's Abbey. And afterwards each relative of the deceased, or the passing friend, or the 'good Christian,' put up a stone or cast a pebble upon one of the little heaps, several of which can still be identified as belonging to particular families.

A modern adaptation of this custom, is the placing of crosses on roadsides to mark the place where a fatal accident happened and by this means remind people to say a prayer for the dead.

Many writers mention the heaps of small stones seen near holy wells. Such a cairn was described at St. Patrick's Well in Kilcorkey parish, Co. Roscommon and another at Tullaghan Well, Co. Sligo. At Tobar Achuma, Clonmore, Co. Roscommon, there is another heap of stones and O'Donovan wrote that each pilgrim added a further stone to the heap as part of the ritual of the pilgrimage. At Tobar-Olla-Breanainn on Valentia Island, there is another cairn of small stones, and Philip Dixon Hardy mentioned this practice at the Struel Wells near Downpatrick, Co. Down. In Moyarta parish, Co. Clare, on a bank above a tidal holy well, there is another heap of small stones and pebbles which were left by the pilgrims, and many references to similar heaps can be found in the *Ordnance Survey Letters*. Two notable cairns mentioned were at St. Bride's Well in

Kilbride parish and at St. Patrick's Well on Downpatrick Head, both in Co. Mayo. St. Buonia's Well in Co. Kerry is 'a beautiful spring around which the pious peasants have raised a large cairn of pebbles the countless records of the rounds which have been paid there for ages.' Many more examples of this widespread practice during pilgrimages to holy wells might be given, but these are typical.

At some wells, there may be a number of such cairns. Morris wrote of a nameless holy well two miles from Milford in Co. Donegal, where there were five such cairns, all made up of the pebbles which had been added by the pilgrims. In some cases, the stones used were specially chosen. On Iniskea South, a small island off the south end of the Mullet peninsula in Co. Mayo there is an ancient church dedicated to St. Dervla, and near it, the saint's well and cairn of stones. In this case the stones making up the cairn are white. At St. Laichteen's Well in Grenagh parish, Co. Cork, to which pilgrims go on St. John's Day, there is a variation of this practice. A reference to this well reads:

> An old woman attends here on the day of the patron saint and deposits white stones in the water which flows off from the well as forfeits for those who come for cures to this place.

White stones are also mentioned in a description of the pilgrimage to Tobar Aibheog in Co. Donegal.

It is tempting to speculate about the reason for this practice of leaving a stone at the holy well. It might be thought of as a reminder to the saint that the pilgrim had done him honour by visiting his holy well, or it might be a way of saying that the pilgrim would wish to remain at the holy place. In my opinion, the stones were substitutes for gifts to the saint: most people were too poor to afford a real gift, so the stone took the place of a material gift.

SPECIAL STONES

Some stones have been credited with very special powers. Plummer mentioned amber coloured stones from the saint's well which protected the possessors against losses due to fire or water.

About three quarters of a mile north of Drumcullin Abbey, in Co. Offaly, are St. John's Well and St. John's Stone. This stone is visited by pilgrims on St. John's Day and:

> The stone is a large virgin rock, five feet high and eight or nine feet long. The deep crevices in it, and the ground about it are

strewn with the most varied objects, rosary beads, little devotional images and cards, buttons of all kinds down to the linen variety, clasps, brooches, pipe bowls, even money. These objects were accounted for by a little girl of the locality. 'If you say a prayer at the rock and leave something there, you leave your sins behind you.'

Another such stone was found on the seashore near Kilrush, Co. Clare, and was described by Shaw-Mason as:

> A stone upon which Senanus once knelt and in which the print of his knee is still shown at the head of the creek at Kilrush is still held in such veneration that every countryman who passes it, bows, takes off his hat or mutters a prayer as he goes along.

This reverence for a special stone is not unusual, and the custom of saying a short prayer at certain places was found all over Ireland. It was the practice that people passing a graveyard or a church would take off their hats and say a few prayers as they went and, as has been mentioned, people prayed at heaps of stones by the wayside. The power over stones, attributed to St. Senan, extended to all the stones on his holy island, Inis Cathaigh, and it was believed that a stone from the island, if kept on board a boat, was able to preserve it from danger. As an additional safety measure, it was the practice to sail the boat on its first voyage round the holy island, to ensure the protection of the saint for the boat and its crew.

Perhaps the most elaborate of all the rituals to honour these special stones is that connected with the pilgrimage to the well near the ruins of St. Mary's Priory of Canons Regular of St. Augustine at Dungiven, Co. Derry. The pilgrimage was described in some detail by the Reverend Alexander Ross, Church of Ireland Rector of the parish. He wrote:

> Early almost every Sunday morning from Patrick's Day to about Michaelmas a number of devotees surround this well and after bowing towards it with great reverence, walk around it a certain number of times, repeating during their progress, a stated measure of prayer, then they wash their hands and feet with water, and tear off a small rag from their clothes which they tie on a bush, overhanging the well – from thence they all proceed to a large stone in the River Roe, immediately below the old church and having performed an ablution they walk around the stone bowing to it, and repeating prayers as at the well. The next movement is to the old church within which a similar ceremony goes on and they finish this rite, by a procession and prayer round

the upright stone already described.

The stone to which the writer refers is a pillar stone called Cloch-Patrick which is about ten feet high and stands in a prehistoric barrow about 300 yards east of the old church.

A pillar stone near St. Adamnan's well at Temple Moyle in Cloncha parish, Co. Donegal, was mentioned by Morris in his study of Donegal holy wells. Pilgrims seeking a cure went first round the well and then rubbed the diseased part against the pillar stone. Morris said that at the time he wrote the stone had been destroyed.

There seems to be a little doubt that these stones were treated as idols, even though the devotion had been covered with a thin veneer of Christianity. It is impossible now to trace the origin and history of these practices in any detail and no effort will be made to do so, but it is indeed remarkable that the practice managed to survive fifteen hundred years of Christianity.

STONES WHICH RETURN HOME

Stones with the strange power of returning home are found in most parts of Ireland. Two such stones were described by John O'Donovan in the old graveyard at Kilultagh in Co. Roscommon. They were rounded stones and were believed to mark the graves of two ecclesiastics and the story was that if ever they were taken away they always came back uninjured. O'Donovan did not tell a story to explain why the stones were given such power.

Another stone with even more wonderful powers may be found near Tobar na Mult at Ardfert, Co. Kerry. This is a great heavy slab which may have once been part of an altar tomb and the story is that an enemy (Cromwellian) once used an ox cart to take it away from the well. When the cart had got as far as Bullock Hill, it stopped and the oxen refused to move it any further, so it was left on the spot until the next morning. Then, to the surprise of some people, the stone was found to have moved back to its original place near the well.

Another story tells of a fisherman who took a stone from the ruined wall of Gorman church near Malin Head, Co. Donegal. He put the stone into his boat intending to use it as a floating anchor but when he put it overboard, off Inishtrahull, it seemed to get loose from the rope which was attached to it and, apparently, sank. When he got home, he found that the stone was back in its place in the church wall. This power of locomotion is one of the many extraordinary powers possessed by a stone called 'the Cappeen Olan' which has been mentioned a number of times. This was in Coolineagh townland in Aghabulloge parish, Co. Cork and it was believed that it would always return home, no matter how far it had been removed. Another homing stone was described in Cappanagrown townland in Aghinagh parish, Co. Cork. It is a large flat stone containing a *bullan* near a well called Tobar a'Noonan which is not thought of as a holy well. In this case the stone, which is very large and heavy, was removed and built into a wall, but was found back at the well in the morning.

Still another such Co. Cork stone was described in the *Journal of the Cork Historical and Archaeological Society*. In describing St. Brigid's Church, Loch Hyne, Co. Cork, the writer said:

> 50 yards north east of the church is a portion of a broken pillar stone 18″ × 15½″ with an incised cross . . . It is said that once when it was carried off by a sailor, and taken to his home it was found back in its place the next morning. The sailor was drowned shortly afterwards. It is also believed that the part of the stone on which the cross is, cannot be damaged or injured.

Stories of these self moving stones may be heard in every part of Ireland.

FLOATING STONES

Stories of stone boats and stones that float can also be heard in many parts of Ireland. One of these concerns St. Mogue, who was born on an island in Templeport Lake in Co. Cavan. In one version of the story, the new born saint was taken to the mainland for baptism on a large floating flagstone, and according to a second version, the priest who was to baptise the infant crossed to the island on the flagstone. The stone remained and was used to ferry coffins to the island for burial. All went well until a courting couple went out sailing on the stone. At the insult, the stone broke into three parts, and the offending couple were drowned. One part floated to St. Mogue's Island, one to a smaller island in the lake, and the third piece reached the mainland and is now to be seen in the church at Kildoe, where people bless themselves with water which is kept in a hollow in it.

Still more dramatic is the story of St. Boec, whose church is near the seashore at Carnsore Point in the parish of Carn, Co. Wexford. It was said that St. Boec sailed to Brittany on a stone and when he had landed near Penmarch in the parish of Treguenec, the stone returned to Ireland and now lies on the shore near the saint's church just above high water mark. Fortunately, a piece of the stone remained in Brittany and may be seen in a cemetery attached to the saint's chapel there. It bears the imprint of St. Boec's head and sufferers used to come and place their heads on it to be relieved of fever.

St. Boec appears to have specialised in treating cases of fever and it was the custom, in some parts of Brittany, that fever patients touched his missal, in the hope of being cured. In other cases, water which had touched the saint's relics, was drunk by the sufferers and some of it was sprinkled on their foreheads. The stone which lies on the shore of Carn has a cross incised on it but does not, as far as I know, form part of the pilgrimage to Carn church.

At Kilbarry Church, in Co. Roscommon, there is a floating stone which can easily be found. It had long remained on a lake shore but, some years ago, it was taken to the local church were it is kept in the churchyard and referred to as St. Barry's stone boat. It is 8' × 4' × 3' and bears some resemblance to a boat, and is now easily found because a modern statue of St. Barry wearing a green chasuble, has been put on it. The story, as recorded by O'Donovan, says that the saint used it to cross the river Shannon and as long as the people of the district retained their innocence, they continued to use it after his time. Unfortunately, when they lost their innocence, the stone boat sank and as proof of the truth of this story, it can be seen that the stone bears the imprint of St. Barry's knees.

Stories of two more floating stones can be heard around Lough Ree. One of these was provided with a self propelling power and was used to ferry the stones to build the churches on Inis Clothran from the place where they were quarried at Cashel on the eastern shore of the lake. This stone continued to be used until, one day, a man went across to fetch cabbages from the monks' garden on the island. Unfortunately, during the journey, he was suddenly taken ill and found it necessary to perform an office of nature on the stone which instantly sank causing the unfortunate man to be drowned. The second story from Lough Ree concerns a flagstone which was used to ferry bodies to Saints' Island for burial. On one occasion, a woman went to wash clothes in the lake and used the floating stone as a possing stone. It was explained that during the washing, urine was poured on the clothes and this caused the stone to disappear. Still another stone boat can be found on the shore of Loch Allen. This was also used to carry bodies from the mainland to a holy island called Inismagrath, where there are the ruins of an ancient church and a graveyard. I did not learn why this stone has also lost its power to float.

Still another floating stone is that one which saved St. Buadan from his enemies, and now lies on the shore at the mouth of the Culdaff River in Co. Donegal and bears the marks of the saint's five fingers. The story is that St. Columcille and St. Buadan went across to Scotland to preach the gospel, but their mission was not very successful and they were attacked and had to hurry back to their boat. Columcille got first to the boat and pushed it off, leaving Buadan standing on a rock. But all ended happily, because the rock broke off and carried Buadan safely across to Culdaff on the Inishowen peninsula.

Many floating stones are mentioned in the *Lives of the Irish Saints*, but perhaps the most dramatic story of such stone boats comes from the Isle of Skye in Scotland. The story concerns a princess called Scotia, who joined Joseph of Arimathea and a miscellaneous collection of other saints, and they travelled by stone boat from Palestine to Ireland. In Ireland, the boat travelled overland to Tara and then, after a short stay there, on to the Isle of Skye. From there is moved to Iona, where the boat and the saints decided to remain.

HOLED STONES

Holed stones are found all over Ireland, but they appear to be most common in Co. Kerry. Generally, the holes are quite small but in one case, probably the most famous of all these stones, the hole is 3 feet × 2 feet. This stone is the Cloch Liath at Carrow More, Co. Sligo, beside a famous well called Tobar na bhFian, from which a small stream flows. There are many legends about the well, and the stone marks the point at which three parishes meet, but I have not heard of any pilgrimages, cures or any such practices connected with this well or with the stone.

In the parish of Aghade, near Tullow, Co. Carlow, Cloghfoyle (Cloch a Phoil) is marked on the Ordnance map. This is a large flagstone and has a round hole 11.5 inches in diameter in the thickest part of it. Formerly, children were passed through the hole in order to cure or prevent rickets. I do not believe that this is a very old practice, because rickets appears to have been a rare disease in medieval Ireland. There is a legend about a King's son who was chained to the stone by a chain which was passed through the hole, but he managed to break the chain and deal with his enemies.

Some of the stones are the objects of strange beliefs. One is in the ancient cemetery at Castledermot, Co. Kildare. This is a granite slab called 'the swearing stone' and was used by people for swearing upon. In this case, the 5″ circular hole is at the centre of a ringed cross and was described by Lord Walter Fitzgerald. He also described another holed stone at Larghbryan, near Maynooth.

Cloch na Peacaib (Sinners Stone) is at Kilquhone, Co. Cork. John Windle described it as 6′ × 2′4″, 'and of inconsiderable thickness'. In this case, the hole is funnel shaped, wide at one side and tapering to 3″ – 4″ on the other side. Windle said that women, nearing their confinement, used draw cloths through the hole in order to ensure a favourable delivery. Westropp also reported that cloths were passed through a hole in a stone near Monaster Ciarain on Inishmore on the Aran Islands, and the cloths were then used to treat sore limbs. There is a ringed cross in the centre of the stone and the hole, a smaller one, is above the circle. MacAlister suggested that this stone was used as a sundial and the gnomon was attached to the hole.

Another holed stone was found on Inis Cealtra (Holy Island) in Loch Derg. The Stone was at a ruined church called Teampul Caimin and a rude attempt had been made to scratch the outline of a cross around the hole. The holed stone at Kilmalkedar in Co. Kerry, was famous as healing stone.

It was firmly believed by many of the old inhabitants of Kerry that persons afflicted with chronic rheumatism, 'falling sickness', or other ills, might by passing three times round it (with faith and by the offering of certain prayers) be restored to health.

Morris mentioned a holed pillar stone in Glen Columcille, Co. Donegal. On completing the pilgrimage at the holy well there, pilgrims looked through the hole towards the south east and

if they were spiritually in a pure state it was believed they would get a glimpse of heaven. No one gets such a vision now because the people are no longer what they used to be and the class thats going now dont deserve to see such Sights.

In Co. Kerry, at least seven of these holed stones have been described. These are at Kilmalkedar, Doonbeg, Kilabuonia, Aghacorrible in Ardmore townland near Dingle, Reask, Ballinskelligs and Ballyferriter. Those at Reask and Ballyferriter are each in a callura, i.e., a place used to bury unbaptised infants, probably the site of a forgotten church. Those at Kilmalkedar, Kilabuonia and Ballinskelligs are near old monastic sites, and the stones at Doonbeg and Aghacorrible are associated with ancient ring forts.

There is a holed stone inside a large ring fort in Kilcolman parish, Co. Cork.

The farmer of the locality said that if those suffering from any hurt or wrong pass a handkerchief through the hole they would be cured. He also said that, some years ago the owner of the land tilled the fort and set potatoes there. When dug the potatoes were like cabbage stumps and when boiled gave off a strong disagreeable smell.

Many of the holed stones have crosses of different shapes incised on them. In addition to those mentioned, the stone at Reask Co. Kerry has a cross with the perpendicular limbs two and a half times as long as the horizontal limbs. The Ballyferriter stone also has an incised Greek cross with a circle and a long, slender shaft.

It is not possible to do more than guess why these holes were made. They do not appear to have any Christian significance and the crosses which have been incised upon them may have been an effort to christianize them. The fact that similar holed stones are found all over Western Europe and as far east as India, would indicate that they belong to a time well before Christianity. Many of them are found near old monastic or other ancient sites, but this might be explained by saying that some sites which were holy places of the prechristian Irish, were taken over by the Christian missionaries. Clearly, they were of significance to the men who made them, but why they did so cannot now be known. Generally the holed stones only had a minor part in the ritual of visiting holy wells.

BULLAUNS

In all parts of Ireland, stones which bear oval or round depressions are found. In many cases, they are found near old monastic sites and are often the subject of strange beliefs and many legends have been attached to them. They are usually known as *bullauns* or basin stones and in some cases they are even regarded as holy wells, and people say that water is always found in them. O'Donovan had heard this story about bullauns, but despite the story, many of them were found to be dry when he inspected them. There is no written evidence to show why they were made.

Wilde mentioned a number of these stones in his book on Loch Corrib. One of these was kept on the altar in a church called Teampull na Naomh on Inis a'Ghaill in Loch Corrib and another, a double bullaun, was near Teampull Brecain on the west shore of the lake. But the most interesting of them, called Leac na bPoll or the 'flagstone of the holes'

> takes precedence of all other stones in Cong. It is a large triangular red grit flag, two feet thick and eight and a half feet long in its greatest diameter, from under which a never-failing limpid spring issues. Its upper surface is hollowed into five basin-like smooth excavations, averaging twelve inches wide and four and a half deep and usually known as *Bullauns* from the Latin *bulla* a bowl; and which from their being invariably found in immediate connection with the most ancient churches may be regarded as primitive baptismal fonts.

Liam Price who studied the *bullauns*, believed that there were hundreds of them in Ireland and at least thirty of them in or about Glendalough 'and there are nearly as many more in the lands which formerly belonged to the monastery.' In many cases the water found in the bullaun is used to cure diseases, most usually warts, and Lord Walter Fitzgerald described a pilgrimage to what was called The Deer Stone at Glendalough. He said that those seeking a cure must visit the stone on Sunday, Tuesday and Thursday in the same week and at each visit the pilgrim must go seven times round the stone on his bare knees. He also recorded the story of the deer which came and gave her milk into the *bullaun*, in answer to the prayers of the saint. This story is also told about a number of other bullauns.

There is a famous stone, with at least nine bullauns, near Blacklion in Killinagh parish, Co. Cavan. In each of the bullauns there is a rounded stone which more or less fits its place. On a number of occasions, these have been said to be cursing stones and, as part of the cursing ritual, the rounded stones were turned. This is quite unlikely. Such a practice with any other bullaun stones has not been recorded and on a visit to Blacklion, I did not hear that the stones were ever so used.

It is also unlikely that these stones were ever used as baptismal fonts. It is unthinkable that thirty baptismal fonts would be found in Glendalough and, in any case, why would anyone need five baptismal fonts all gouged out of the same stone, even in a holy place like Cong. Price was of opinion that they were used to grind grain and such things and as one got worn deep a new one was formed. As evidence in favour of this, he showed that the stones in which the bullauns are found are large and would be steady during the grinding. He also showed a picture of a flat stone with a bullaun on both sides, one of which was worn into the other. He explained this by saying that when one bullaun got too deep, the stone was turned over and a new bullaun formed and continued in use until it wore through to the bottom of the old one.

Price then went on to discuss the use of these ancient food mixers. He showed pictures of some ancient mortars, and showed that they continued in use in some of the Scottish Islands until the nineteenth century.

SWEARING STONES

As a child, I remember a swearing stone in my native little town, Ballinamore in Co. Leitrim. This was on the top of Canaboe hill. It was a huge stone, at least six feet high and in the shape of a fat man and, on the side facing the street, a rough outline of a cross had been cut. It was used as a swearing stone for people who brought cattle to the fair – since no tolls were paid on cattle which had not been sold. In case of dispute, the collector of the tolls might ask the person in charge of the cattle to place his hand on the stone and declare that the cattle had not been sold. I am told that 'the big stone' has been broken up and removed by an 'improving' local authority.

The 'swearing stone' at Castledermot has already been mentioned. Bishop Dive Downes mentioned a swearing stone in Co. Cork. He wrote:

Monday May 27, 1700. I went to Kineigh: the parish stands three miles distant from Ballimoney to the N.N.W. . . . A high round tower stands in the S.W. corner of the churchyard . . . 'Tis supposed this church was formerly a cathedral. A stone is in the S.W. corner of the church of Kineigh counted very sacred which the Irish solemnly swear upon.

A notable reference to such a stone can be found in Wilde's book on Loch Corrib. He said that the stone, known as Leac Fheichin, was near Maam on the west side of the lake, and had been originally at Tobar Fheichin near the River Dumhachta, a short distance away. The stone, an oval shaped flagstone, was the 'touchstone' and the terror of all evil doers for miles around, for whoever was accused or suspected of a crime was either 'dared to Leac Feichin' or voluntarily underwent the ordeal of turning the flag with certain rites and incantations not now necessary to describe. The *leac* has long disappeared but, in this case, the ritual may have been that the individual who was suspected of or charged with a crime, prayed and turned the oval flagstone in a clockwise direction in proof of the truth of what he said. If he had told the truth all would be well, but if what he said was untrue, then St. Feichin was mortally insulted and was certain to take vengeance on the individual. This was almost universally believed.

Swearing objects were normally such things as the saint's bell or his crozier. These were found in all parts of the country, but most of these objects are now in museums.

CURSING STONES

Cursing stones are mentioned a number of times in the *Ordnance Survey Letters*. One of these stones was kept in the graveyard at the old church in Kilcummin parish, Co. Mayo, and known as Leac Cuimin. It was turned anti-clockwise to bring misfortune on an enemy. O'Connor wrote:

> A man called Mochan used to turn it for pay it is said, who knew the particular way in which it might be done so that the curse might have the effect. He turned it once against a man called Waldron who consequently went mad. A friend of Waldron, the son of Parson Little of Lacken, went and broke the stone but later his father put the bits together. Later Father Lyons took it away and it was built into the cathedral in Ballina. The story went that a piece of the stone remained and continued to be turned.

Some more details about this stone were provided by Westropp. He said that it was used principally for the purpose of invoking maledictions on wrong doers, particularly such as were guilty of grave scandal. It was to families named Mochan the privilege belonged of manipulating this stone, and it would appear from this that O'Mochan was a descendant of the coarb of the parish and, as such, he had learned how to carry out the correct cursing ritual. Westropp went on to say that he had, during the past year (1875), enquired about this cursing stone and found that it was generally believed that a piece of the *leac* remained and continued to be turned, 'but I could not hear of anyone who had even invoked it'.

Another such stone was mentioned in *JRSAI* in 1900. This stone was kept at Kilmoon near Lisdoonvarna, Co. Clare, and it was believed that it could be turned to bring misfortune on an enemy. In preparing for this, the individual first fasted and then 'did' certain turns 'against the sun' and then turned the rounded stone. As a result of all this, and certain appropriate curses, it was believed that the mouth of the victim would be twisted awry. It appears that a farmer was charged at the local Petty Sessions with beating an itinerant woman, and his defence was that she had threatened to turn the stone of Kilmoon against him.

At Dromoland in Co. Armagh, St. Mochua's Wishing Stone was near the saint's holy well. The pilgrim made his wish and in an effort to increase the power of the wish, the stone was turned. It was later removed and buried.

In the parish of Oughaval, Co. Mayo, there was an old church which was said to have been built by St. Columcille. O'Connor, who worked with the Ordnance survey team, heard that near this church there was a flagstone called Leac Choluimb Chille which people were in the habit of 'turning' (i.e., to wish each other bad luck) but he said that it had been broken some time since by a man called Gaughan by order of the priest. At the time O'Connor wrote, Gaughan was ninety-one years old, so the *leac* must have been broken during the early years of the nineteenth century.

There was a famous cursing stone on Caher Island off the coast of Co. Mayo. This is a distinguished holy island and it was believed that it was 'not right' to take anything from it. On the island are the ruins of an ancient church called Teampull Phadruig and on the altar of this church the cursing stone called Leac na Naomh (the Saint's flagstone) was to be found. O'Donovan described it as

Inishmurray, Co. Sligo. In the foreground notice the "cursing altar" with many rounded stones on top. In the background the wall of the cashel is shown with the round top of a clochán. See pp. 141—3.

roundish about 2 feet in diameter and composed of different kinds of stones which appear as though cemented together. It was believed to have great sanctity.

T.W. Rolleston visited the island and wrote a description of it. He said that the *leac* was still on the altar in the church along with a portion of a human skull, and a clutter of votive offerings, fish hooks, pence, halfpence, bootlace, grains of shot etc. He was able to take a photograph of the altar which showed part of the *leac*, and the conglomerate structure of it could easily be seen in the photograph.

O'Donovan gave a detailed description of the ritual practiced by people who had recourse to the *leac*. The individual first fasted and prayed at home for a fixed time, asking God, through the intercession of St. Patrick and the other saints to show some sign that the individual had been wronged. He then went over to Caher Island and turned the flagstone against the person who had wronged him. When this had been done, it was believed that storms and hurricanes would occur, causing great destruction of boats and currachs, and in all the destruction some misfortune would befall the wrong doer. In this way it was said that God, or St. Patrick, would show that the suppliant had been wronged and so have his good name vindicated.

References to some other cursing stones can also be found in the *Ordnance Survey Letters*. One of these was called the Claidhmhin Chathasaigh (St. Cathasach's Little Sword) and another was called Leac na Seacht n-Inghion (The Flagstone of the Seven Daughters), but the belief and ritual connected with them are not remembered in any detail.

IDOLS

Perhaps the most extraordinary of these stones is known as 'the god-stone' which is in Granish about a mile from the end of the Beara Peninsula in West Cork. It may be found on a farm belonging to a family called MacCarthy and people have always been reluctant to speak about it until a local priest, who was interested in archaeology, discovered it. There is a vague story about a custom of dressing the stone at certain times of the year, but it is difficult to confirm this.

In any case the experts do not agree about it. Some say it is just a wave washed rock, but it seems that however it may have been moulded by the waves it has also been shaped to resemble a human head and body.

IX

Votive Offerings

The custom of leaving a votive offering is an essential part of a pilgrimage to a holy well. This has certainly been the practice for hundreds of years, and like so many of these practices may go back to the ancient religion of the Celts. Whatever may be said about this, it is well known that during the Middle Ages when rich people went on pilgrimages to famous shrines and such places they were expected to, and did, make offerings, and there is no doubt that some shrines got rich on the offerings of pilgrims. In this country the shrine of Our Lady of Trim became so rich in this way that its wealth provoked the greed of some people at the Reformation. These offerings were not peculiar to Western Europe, or to Christianity and as a child I have often heard old soldiers tell of the offerings made by pilgrims at holy places in India.

During some of the difficult years of the seventeenth and eighteenth centuries it would almost be natural that the people of the parish, and of the neighbourhood, when they assembled at a holy well on the feast day of the patron saint, to make a collection for the priest. At that time the priest may have lived in hiding and there was no way in which he could collect the tithes of his parish, so in order to live he relied on the gifts of his flock. These collections were also made at weddings and funerals, and only recently has the custom of paying funeral offerings come to an end in some parts of the country. I remember seeing a box for offerings in the old graveyard in my native parish on the station day and, in later years, when the box was no longer there, people still left pennies on the ground where it had been, near a stone on which a human face had been carved. The coins were later collected by the parish priest.

References to such collection boxes are rare. One is mentioned at St. Patrick's Well at Sheeplands East, Lecale, Co. Down, and I saw one some months ago near St. Lassair's Well at Kilronan, Co. Roscommon. A considerable amount of work has recently been

113

carried out around this well and the collection box appeared to be one way of trying to pay for the work. In a leaflet giving instructions about the ritual of the pilgrimage to Inish Caol, off the coast of Donegal, it is ordered by the parish priest that no money offerings be left on the holy island. At Ireland's most notable pilgrimages, Cruach Patrick and Loch Derg, no money offerings are given or expected.

Philip Dixon Hardy, whose book on the *Holy Wells of Ireland* reads like a barrister's brief for the prosecution, quotes at length a letter from Father Charles O'Connor to his brother Owen, who was O'Connor Don, (i.e. the head of his family) at the time. It will be realised that as the brother of O'Connor Don, as a Catholic priest and as an Irish speaker, Father O'Connor was certain to be told the truth by everyone in Co. Roscommon who knew him. He wrote:

> I have often enquired of your tenants what they themselves thought of their pilgrimages to the wells of Kil-Archt, Tobar – Brighde, Tobar Muire near Elphin, and Moore near Castlereagh where multitudes assembled annually to celebrate what they in broken English termed Pattrons (Patron's Days): and when I pressed a very old man, Owen Hester, to state what possible advantage he expected to derive from the singular custom of frequenting in particular such wells as were contiguous to an old blasted oak or an upright unhewn stone and what the meaning was of the yet more singular custom of sticking rags on the branches of such trees and spitting on them – his answer, and the answer of the oldest men, was that their ancestors always did it: that it was a preservative against *Geasu-Draoidacht,* i.e. the sorceries of the druids: that their cattle were preserved by it, from infections and disorders: that the *daoini maethe,* i.e. the fairies, were kept in good humour by it: and so thoroughly persuaded were they of the sanctity of those pagan practices that they would travel bareheaded and barefooted from ten to twenty miles for the purpose of crawling on their knees round these wells, and upright stones and oak trees westward as the sun travels, some three times, some six, some nine, and so on, in uneven numbers until their voluntary penances were completely fulfilled.

This letter is especially valuable for anyone wishing to understand this practice of visiting holy wells. Its value is, that it was written by a hostile witness, but one who was in the best possible position to learn what people thought about the practice. It is difficult to be patient with O'Connor, but it must be remembered that during the nineteenth century this attitude was that of many of the leaders of the Catholic Church in Ireland. At that time people were busy working for and looking forward to the day when they would be enlightened and free from all the childish beliefs of the past: some are still looking for this brave new world. As so often happens O'Connor in his efforts to disparage the custom of visiting holy wells, provided a valuable piece of evidence when he mentioned the custom of spitting on the votive offering which I have not found elsewhere. Spittle is regarded as something very personal, and renders the object very personal indeed.

At some pilgrimages a relic of the saint might be taken to the site on the Pattern day and used to bless the pilgrims, and at Cruach Patrick this ancient custom was described in detail by John O'Donovan. At that time, the relic, St. Patrick's Bell, known as the Clog Geal (Bright Bell) was kept in the neighbourhood and was taken to the holy mountain for the pilgrimage. The bell had been originally 'white as snow and brighter than polished silver', but had become black because the demons of the Reek had attacked and pelted it. Those who wished to be blessed by the bell first kissed the cross on it. It was then passed three times, clockwise, round the body of the suppliant by the keeper of the bell who probably said some prayers as he did so. O'Donovan was able to learn that a fee was paid to the keeper of the bell for this service, and in a good season the offerings amounted to £7 – £10, a significant sum in pre-famine Ireland.

On Inis Caoil off the coast of Co. Donegal the pilgrimage season extends from 22nd of May, St. Connal's Day, to the 12th of September. The saint's bell, called the Bearnan (the Gapped Bell of St. Connal Caol) was taken to the pilgrimage island by its keeper, and according to one story, the keeper kept calling to the crowd of the pilgrims saying 'Pay your half-penny and kiss the Bearnan'. This was thought unseemly and the story ends by saying that the keeper of the bell bought sheep with the money of the offerings, but the sheep all died.

These are the only two instances of which I have heard where a significant amount of money passed at a pilgrimage. Probably there were others, but they must have been rare, because the many nineteenth century writers who were bitterly opposed to the practice of visiting holy wells, would have said so, and would have used such a piece of evidence to damn them further. It will be remembered that in many cases, the saints' bells and other such relics, were used to swear upon and in such cases a small fee was paid to the keeper of the relic.

The most usual objects left by pilgrims were the small pieces of cloth which were hung on the saint's tree near the well and in Co. Dublin a holy well is known as a 'rag well.' Nowadays the cloths may be any colour, and nobody pays much attention to the colours, but most of the older references speak of them as multicoloured. At St. Patrick's Well in Mullaghorn parish Co. Cavan, the pieces of cloth were and, I believe still are, red, although some of them have weathered to dull grey. At St. Bernard's Well in Rathbran parish Co. Carlow people remembered many pieces of red flannel being left as votive offerings.

Even today many of the pieces of cloth seen are, or have once been, red. It would seem that the older practice was to use red cloth and to some extent this is still so, but this was not the practice everywhere and a careful examination of the pieces of cloth attached to the iron railing around St. Barry's Well at Kilbarry, Co. Roscommon, showed that they were all white. Red is a colour which is much used for all sorts of magical purposes. It is the colour which is believed to resist the power of evil spirits and it was not unusual to see pieces of red cloth tied on the tails of cattle to protect them against unspecified dangers. The custom of putting a piece of copper wire through the loose skin of the dewlap of cattle is perhaps a similar device and the use of red flannel in folk medicine is also an example of this very ancient belief in the power of red things. This would agree with what Father Charles O'Connor said about the benefits which followed a pilgrimage to a holy well and explain why so many of the pieces of cloth were red.

At some wells pilgrims who sought a cure of any ailment often bathed the diseased part with the water of the well. When this had been done the cloth which had been used for the bathing was attached to the bush as a votive offering. This was done at the holy wells at Diswellstown and at Bridewell, both in Co. Dublin. At St. Patrick's Well at Sheepland East, Locale, Co. Down, the water was used to treat sores on the body. The sores were bathed in the water of the stream which flows from the well – the well water was drunk by the pilgrims – and the cloth used for the bathing was allowed to run off in the stream.

Ordinarily things left as votive offerings were simple personal possessions. As well as pieces of clothing, they include coins, buttons, brooches and other trinkets, pipes, hair pins and many other types of pins, nails, screws and fish-hooks. At a visit to the famous holy whitethorn at Seir Ciaran in Co. Offaly in 1974 I found a strange selection of objects attached to the tree. There were among other things, a clothes peg, a metal corkscrew bottle-opener combined, a string of elastic, female, and a baby's soother. There were also the usual pious bits and pieces that are so well known in Ireland, small crosses, medals, scapulars, fragments of rosary beads, etc. (See p. 95 for illustration).

Sometimes the offerings were left on the ground near the well, or they may be thrown into the well, and I remember as a child seeing a heap of mud which had been taken out of a well; mixed with the mud were numbers of medals, crosses, bits of rosary beads and other such things. While visiting Tobar Mhuire, near Elphin, I noticed that there was only one votive offering to be seen – a small plastic statue of Our Lady, which was placed over the well. On enquiry I learned that at this well it was the custom to put the offerings in a hole in the bank over the well, where I found a large number of them. Money is still left but now the coins are not of significant value. They are sometimes beaten into the trunk of the tree, but more usually remain scattered around the well, and it is said that if anyone were to collect them for his own use he would get the disease which had been left behind by the pilgrim who had left the coin.

Crutches and sticks and such helps have often been left at holy wells by grateful pilgrims who no longer needed them. I have seen these many times, e.g. at Dabhach Bhride, Liscannor, Co. Clare, and at Father Moore's Well at the Curragh of Kildare. Danaher mentioned the case of a man who was lame and needed crutches to walk. Following a visit to St. Colman's Well in Colmanswell parish in Co. Limerick he found he was cured and left his crutches at the well but later he repented of his generosity and took the crutches back to sell them. He again became lame. St. Colman was not one to trifle with, and once when a man worked to earn money on St. Colman's pattern day the money vanished from his pocket as he went past the well.

Tobar an Ratha Bhain at Mashanaglas, Co. Cork, is well known as a healing well. It was especially efficacious in treating rheumatism and formerly very large numbers of crutches could be seen there. One grateful pilgrim, a man called Michael Loney, placed a box containing statues and other pious objects at the well. Another was St. Fursey's Well in Clonmeen parish near Banteer also in Co. Cork. When the 'rounds' had been completed at the well, the pilgrims went and prayed in the church at Banteer. In former times there were so many crutches left at the well that it was popularly known as Tobar Ursa (Ursa i.e. a crutch). The most famous holy well in Co. Donegal was Doon Well in the Kilmacrennan parish and many crutches and sticks were left at it by the pilgrims.

In Co. Carlow O'Toole has described a number of holy wells where crutches were left as votive offerings. One of these was called Killoughternane Well in Sliguff parish, near the ruins of a very ancient church. This well had the honour of being lost and rediscovered about the year 1889, and following the rediscovery, it became a popular well and many cures were claimed. The well might be visited on any Sunday and O'Toole heard that at the time the ancient church was 'filled' with crutches. Formerly crutches were left at St. Martin's Well where a pattern was held on St. Martin's Day. This well was at Cronelea in Mullinacuff. It was the custom to take home water from this well on St. Martin's Day and drink it the same night.

The custom of leaving crutches at two other holy wells was also mentioned by O'Toole in his study of the Holy Wells of Co. Carlow. These were John's Well in Kiltegan parish where a pattern was held on St. John's Eve, and St. Bernard's Well at Rampere in Rathbran parish where a great pattern was held on 20th of August. The pattern was stopped about the year 1800 but even in the third decade of the 20th century people remembered the crutches which had been left at the well.

Leaving a crutch or a stick which a patient was known to have needed and used for some time is a dramatic gesture and as such would appeal to people. Then the pilgrim might identify his crutch with the disability which caused him to need the crutch, so he might hope to get rid of the disability by getting rid of the crutch. I have known a father who continuously ordered his son, who had poliomyelitis and needed the crutch, to discard it. Perhaps in many of these cases which were cured at the holy well it was the excitement of the pattern and the whiskey which was available, which might bring about the apparent cure, rather than the power of the saint. I have known of a number of such whiskey induced 'cures' of rheumatism. Crutches are rarely used by patients nowadays, and it is unlikely that in future many will be left at holy wells.

The most permanent votive offerings are the heaps of small stones, which are sometimes seen at holy wells. Each stone in the heap, and some heaps are very large, has been added by a pilgrim, as a votive offering, and while most votive offerings gradually disappear the stones remain as a permanent memorial to the piety of the pilgrims. The custom is more common along the west coast of Ireland, and in some cases the stones are put into the well.

Pins and nails are often left as votive offerings. At St. Bernard's Well in Rathkeale parish the visits are paid on 20th of August and on Good Friday, and the pilgrims sometimes drive nails into the trunk of the ash tree over the well. Whether this is a reference to the Crucifixion or not, is not clear. At the old church in Kilgeever it was the custom to leave nails in two niches in the east wall and it has been reported that pins and nails were formerly driven into the trunk of the sacred tree of Arboe in Co. Tyrone.

Pins are left at many holy wells. They may be left at St. Boey's Well in Inismagrath parish Co. Leitrim, where they are most often left by pilgrims seeking relief from toothache. Pins are also left in the mortar joints of St. Finan's Church at Killemlagh, Co. Kerry, near the shore of St. Finan's Bay. At some wart wells, it is the practice to lift a little water on the point of a pin and drop it onto the wart, and when this has been done the pin is placed in the water to rust away and it is believed that as the pin rusts away the wart will disappear.

In the *Ulster Journal of Archaeology* Vol. 11–12, a number of what are called pin wells are mentioned. These include Sunday Well at Ballybot, Co. Armagh, where pins were dropped into the water. At Coney Island, also in Co. Armagh was the Pin Well. This 'well' was the pool of water which had accumulated in the fork of a tree. In this case the pins were stuck in the bark of the tree, and there was a similar tree well at Magherinagaw, Co. Antrim, where pins were also stuck in the bark. Pins are dropped into the holy well of Ballyoran in Co. Armagh, but there is a more unusual belief at Glenoran Well, at Teemore Co. Armagh. This well has a sandy bottom through which the water bubbles, and as the pins sink to the bottom, they are carefully watched to see how they will settle on the sandy bottom. This is used as a method of foretelling the future.

Some unusual votive offerings are mentioned. St. Ultan's Well near Baileborough, Co. Cavan, is a popular well and is visited on Christmas Eve, by people carrying candles which do not blow out. Candles were also left at the Rag Well at Diswellstown, Co. Dublin, on the pilgrimage day, May Eve, and lately some candles were left at Our Lady's Well, at Mulhuddart, Co. Dublin. They had been left there on the 8th of September, the pilgrimage day, and I saw them a few days later. In Kilmurry parish Co. Limerick the holy well is dedicated to St. Mary Magdalen. Rounds are made on her feast day, 22nd July, and flowers and candles are left at the well.

At St. Buonia's Well at Kilabuonia, in Co. Kerry, the votive offerings are pushed through a hole in one of the stones 'surrounding the priest's grave' near the well. Locks of hair are left at Tobar Keelagh not far from Tourmakeady, Co. Mayo, and pieces of broken china were left at St. Luctigern's Well at Fenloe in Co. Clare. Similarly broken cups were left at the grave of Fr. John

O'Callaghan in Aghinagh parish Co. Cork. Part of the ritual here was to take water from the holy well in a cup and then a little earth from Father O'Callaghan's grave is added to the water. If the complaint from which the pilgrim suffers is external the mixture is applied to it, and if it is internal the mixture is drunk. The cup used is then left as a votive offering. St. Brigid's Well at Castlemagner is well known as a healing well and people used to travel long distances to drink the well water and then leave the drinking vessels at the well.

There have been many reasons put forward to explain this widespread practice. It may be that the practice began by the pilgrims bringing a gift to the god or to the priest of the god, who was in charge of the holy place. This seems to be a reasonable suggestion – it is the obvious and natural thing to do especially by people who went to the holy place seeking some benefit. It would also be reasonable to believe that a grateful pilgrim should return and bring an offering when his request had been granted.

The leaving of such things as crutches and sticks, appears to be the action of the grateful pilgrim who had been restored to health and had no further need for his crutch. Similarly the pious objects might have been left as continuing prayers. Often such things as pins, nails, needles, and fish-hooks are left. These might be thought of as representing the pain or illness from which the pilgrim was seeking relief. As the objects left are of little value they must have had some symbolic value and some reasons for leaving them have been suggested.

X

Fish in Holy Wells

Sacred supernatural fish are found in many countries, and are not in any way peculiar to Ireland. If a person believes in the sanctity and healing power of the water of the well, it will follow that any fish found in the well must be supernatural. In Irish mythology stories of such wonderful fish can be found. The best known of these is the story of the Salmon of Knowledge, and how Fionn Mac Cumhaill, set to watch it as it grilled, touched it with his thumb and thrust the burned thumb into his mouth and in this way came to share the knowledge of the salmon. In the Lives of the Irish Saints some other legendary stories of fish can be found. One of these tells of the great fish which was found by St. Enda at Lemchoill in the Aran Islands and another tells of the miraculous fish which St. Patrick caught in a dry field at Ardagh in Co. Longford.

A more historical reference to these sacred fish can be found in the *Annals of the Four Masters* in the year 1061. It reads:

> An army was led by Aedh an Gha-bhearnaigh O'Connor to Kincora: and he demolished the fortress and destroyed the enclosing wall of the well and ate its two salmons, and also burned Killaloe.

There is no reason to doubt the accuracy of this entry. The destruction of Kincora, which was the chief fortress of his enemies, the O'Briens, would be thought of as usual but the burning of the holy place of the tribe, Killaloe, and the killing and eating of the sacred salmon would be seen as mortal insults and sacrilege.

During the last two centuries there have been many references to these special fish and they have been seen at different times by very reliable witnesses, in wells in different parts of the country. Usually they are believed to be immortal and indestructible, and often a story is provided to prove this. Perhaps the best documented of these concerns a natural cave in the limestone between Loch Mask

121

and Loch Corrib. The cave, known as Poll na gColum, from the large numbers of pigeons found roosting in it, is entered by a flight of steps which lead down to an underground river, to which women went to draw water or to wash clothes. A trout which was not known to take bait was occasionally seen in the water, and had dark markings on its side – believed to be due to the marks of a gridiron. The story was that an enemy (unbelieving yeoman) caught the trout and set it to cook on a gridiron. When he touched the fish with his sword, it turned into a beautiful woman, who then disappeared and the trout was found next day back in the water and showing on its side the dark lines made by the hot gridiron.

Wakeman visited Poll na gColum about 1879 and observed the dark markings on the trout. He also recorded the story of a certain doctor called Ball who wished to demonstrate his scientific unbelief in such superstitions by shooting the trout. When the time of the trial came, the light was just right and the doctor and the other people who had gathered there could see the trout clearly. As the doctor fired, a cloud obscured the sun and when the smoke cleared away, there was the trout obviously unharmed. Wakeman added that the onlookers had been greatly disturbed by the doctor's action, and went away convinced that the cloud had been sent to protect the sacred fish.

Wakeman also visited St. Ciaran's Well three miles west of Kells in Co. Meath and was also able to see the sacred trout there. Some further details are given by Mac Néill who said that three trout were believed to appear in the well at midnight before the first Sunday in August. They remained for a few moments and then disappeared until the following year. In a recent visit to Castlekeeran, I met a man who said he had often spent the night before the station day at the well and had seen two trout, both of which swam round in the shape of a celtic cross before they disappeared.

The evidence in these two cases leaves no doubt that real fish have been seen in the wells, and it is also certain that fish lived in some other wells. It is however possible to doubt the literal truth of the stories in some cases, and it may be a little unfair to wonder how fish could be seen in a well at midnight, no matter how holy the well or the season.

In Dingle parish Co. Kerry, a holy well called Tobar Monachan was very popular during the nineteenth century. It was visited on Sundays all through the year and had a great reputation as a healing well. It was believed that a salmon and an eel lived in the well, and if a pilgrim managed to see them this was taken to mean that the pilgrim would have his request granted. Here again one may doubt that a salmon or an eel lived in the well, but everyone remembers the size of the fish that got away and it is easy to see what a bright Kerry intelligence would make of a pair of minnows.

Another Co. Kerry well, St. Dathalan's at Ballyheig, is believed to contain a sacred trout. In this case, an enemy (Crosby his name) set his two dogs to go into the well and attack the trout. When the dogs came out of the well, they attacked and savaged the enemy, and as a consequence he went mad and stank until the day he died.

John O'Donovan gave some details about the fish which lived in Brideswell, Co. Roscommon. Two trout had lived in the well until about sixteen years before his visit in 1836. Formerly one of the trout had been caught, and like the trout taken from Poll na gColum, was put on a gridiron to cook. When it felt the heat, it flew off and returned to the well, where it continued for several years with the marks of the gridiron clearly seen on its side. Finally, a boy caught and ate one of the trout 'to his own destruction' and a child caught the other one. O'Donovan also mentioned another trout in a well in Tarmon townland near Boyle.

Even in Co. Dublin some holy wells were believed to contain sacred fish. Wakeman mentioned one of these, which he called Jacob's Well. It was 'between Monkstown and Kingstown' and contained 'a mysterious and sacred trout'. Another Dublin holy well near Tallaght had a reputation for curing headaches and indigestion. It was closed up by the owner of the land, a man called O'Neil, but it broke out at the opposite side of the field, and the waters continued to relieve the sufferers who came to it. Unfortunately the trout which had been seen in the old well did not appear in the new one.

In Co. Cork in Walshestown in the parish of Athnowen, there are two adjoining wells, called Sunday's Well and Mary's Well, and stations are performed at both wells as parts of the pilgrimage. Formerly there was a trout in Mary's Well and an eel in Sunday's Well. In this case, the story is of a woman, a stranger to the district, who took some water from Mary's Well, which she used to boil potatoes. As usual, the water would not boil and when her husband learned what she had done he emptied the water into a bucket and found the eel. Even though he took care to put the eel back in the well, it soon dried up. Mention is also made of sacred fish in St. Brigid's Well at Birchfield, on the estate of a certain Cornelius O'Brien. The well was believed to house one large eel and eleven small eels which could only be seen at certain times during the year. Some water was taken from the well but it could not be boiled and was found to contain one of the small eels.

The Holy Wells of Ireland

In an article on the Holy Wells of Donegal, Henry Morris wrote:

In many of the wells where stations are still performed it is believed there is a trout or more generally two that have lived in the well from time immemorial. Every person cannot see these trout; they reveal themselves only to certain people and it is believed to be a highly propitious omen for the person who sees them. It is considered unlucky to interfere with them. There is a story told of an unbeliever who netted one of the trout, brought it home and put it on a gridiron to broil. But in a twinkling it disappeared and next day was found swimming in the well as before.

In the *Life of St. Columcille*, there is a story which may have been the source of some later legends. It said that the saint, when a child, was given a dead trout, which he restored to life and put into the well, where it continued to live. If at any time the fish was caught, and taken away from the well, the water could not be boiled until it was put back again.

Danaher, in writing of the Holy Wells of Limerick, also tells of the sacred fish. In Askeaton parish in the townland called Moig South there are two holy wells in one of which lives a special trout. In Nautenan parish in a townland called Ardgrove South is St. James' Well which is visited on the 25th of July, St. James' Day. The water of the well is believed to cure sore eyes, and sores on the skin, and if the pilgrim manages to see the fish, the cure is certain. Danaher also records the same story about the trout which was said to live in Lady's Well in Ballylanders parish, Co. Kerry. Two other Co. Kerry wells were said to contain everlasting trout. These were St. Nicholas' Well in Ballyduff parish, and Tobar na Mult in Ardfert parish.

In the parish of Oughaval in Co. Mayo, there is an old church which is said to have been built by St. Columcille. O'Donovan reported that the saint blessed the well, near this old church, which is a famous healing well, but unless the pilgrim is able to see the three trout in the water the disease is not curable.

The story of the magic fish is told about Tobar an Ailt on the shore of Lough Gill, in Co. Sligo. Even more famous is the well at Tullaghan, also in Co. Sligo, of which many legends are recorded, including one about a sacred trout.

A variation of the story was recorded by John O'Donovan from Kilallan parish in Co. Westmeath. It happened that the water of a holy well there was disturbed and made muddy by a rustic. When this happened, three croziers in the shape of eels came out of the

Entrance to the grove around Tobar an Ailt, Co. Sligo.

well and flew off in different directions. The rustic managed to hit one of the three which fell to the ground and expired. It was taken from the rustic by a nobleman, when it was found to be a crozier with a head shaped like an eel. Also the neck of the crozier was found to be damaged and this was said to have been caused by the blow of the rustic. It was called the Bachal Gholain and like many such relics was used for swearing upon.

This story may have been told to give a special power to the crozier and the story-teller began with the desecration of the well by the rustic. He then brought in the legend of the sacred fish, with which his hearers were familiar, and as final proof added the evidence of the eel shape of the head and the damage to its neck.

Sacred fish have been honoured in many countries in Europe, Africa and Asia. This would follow the well worship which is part of natural religion, and is much too big a subject to be discussed here. However, it is necessary to mention the belief in the sacred fish which were found in some holy wells in Wales. As in Ireland, the fish are either trout or eels. In one case, Ffynnon Beris in Caernarvanshire, the trout were quite famous and it was thought to indicate a favourable prognosis if they were seen by a patient bathing in the well. Trout were also seen in Ffynnon Winnog in Cardiganshire, and Lhuyd mentioned the trout which were in a holy well called Ffynnon Gwyfan, near Disserth church in Flintshire.

Sacred eels also were found in many wells. At Ffynnon Gybi in Caernarvanshire, the patient stood in the well and it was believed that a cure was a certain if the eel which lived there, came and wrapped itself around his legs. In Anglesea, the movements of the sacred eels which lived in Fynnon Ddwynwen indicated the matrimonial prospects of those who visited the well. These and some others were described by Francis Jones in his book, *The Holy Wells of Wales*.

A variation of this story of sacred fish was heard by my friend, Mr. M.J. Molloy to whom this book is dedicated. His informant, a nun, recalled that twenty-five years ago, many members of her community used visit St. Patrick's Well near Ballyhaunis on the pattern day. Sometimes they were forced to remain at the well for some hours until the Reverend Mother at last managed to see an immortal frog which lived in the well. To see this frog was a sure sign that her request would be granted.

XI

Domestic Animals at Holy Wells

As might be expected, there were many practices designed to protect the cattle against all sorts of dangers, real or imaginary, and often the local saint was invoked to help in these, as in so many other cases. All possible measures were taken to keep the cattle healthy and to increase their milk yield and their fertility. Some measures were also taken to protect the horses and other domestic animals, but the cattle were more important than all the others, reflecting their importance in the Irish economy. The most usual method of protecting the cattle was to swim them in the sea or in some lake or river.

At Clonmany on the Inishowen Peninsula, pilgrims went to St. Columcille's Well on the sea shore there on his feast day, the 9th of June. Early in the 19th century we get:

> They formerly drove their cattle to the beach on that day and swam them in that part of the sea into which runs the water of St. Columb's Well which is thereby made holy water: but this custom of late has not been practiced.

This well was also mentioned by Henry Morris. He said that it had the additional virtue of being covered at full tide, and of containing fresh water when the tide was out, as well as a cure for infertility in the cows.

Morris reported a similar practice from the same district in Donegal. The Culdaff River enters the sea at a small village called Bunagee, in the north of Inishowen. A deep pool called 'the Leamy' in this river is regarded as a holy well and Morris reported that formerly any cattle which had been bitten by a dog were made to swim in 'the Leamy' as a method of preventing madness. When this had been done and the animal had come out of the pool, it was found to be normally quiet or had become completely mad. In such a case, it was immediately shot and Morris said that he had spoken to a man who had seen this happen.

Gougan Lake, the source of the River Lee, was the site of a famous pilgrimage on 23rd – 24th of June. This was described in detail by Crofton Croker and quoted by Dixon Hardy. The centre of the pilgrimage is a holy island now joined to the mainland by a causeway. At the time of the pilgrimage, people drove their cattle through the water of a part of the lake as a method of preventing the murrain. When this had been done, the spancels of the cattle were taken and hung on a large wooden pole which stood in the centre of an enclosure on the holy island. It is likely that the pole had replaced a sacred tree.

The same practice was carried out at Devinish, a holy island in Lower Lough Erne in Co. Fermanagh. Early in the nineteenth century a hostile witness wrote a description of the pilgrimage to Devinish on St. Molaise's Day, the 12th of September, and continued:

> On the North East side of Devenish is a bay called the Cooey. If cattle infected with murrain (blackleg, etc. etc.) be driven through the same, they are exempted that season as is often experienced.

It would appear that the writer of this account, even though he did not believe in the power of the pilgrimage to relieve such things as backache, did believe in the efficacy of swimming the cattle in the Cooey.

In the *Ordnance Survey Letters* from Co. Clare, O'Curry mentioned a small lake called Loch Iona in Dysert parish. He said that it was the custom to drive sick cattle through the water of this lake 'for the recovery of their health' and added that this might be done on any Monday or Thursday.

Another example of this ancient practice has been described from the parish of Burrishoole, Co. Mayo. In the *Ordnance Survey Letters*, O'Donovan recorded a legend about St. Brigid quarrelling with the local saint, Marcan. When pilgrims visited Loch Marcan, some of them drove their cattle there to be cured of their diseases by swimming them in the lake. However, on the journey to Loch Marcan, they must be very careful to avoid Kilbride, or any other place sacred to St. Brigid, lest she undo the favourable results of the pilgrimage, because St. Brigid remembers the quarrel and she 'does not wish that St. Marcan should get credit for any miracles'. It will be remembered that St. Brigid is often represented with a cow in her arms and in many of the stories about her she is said to protect the cattle.

128

Wilde gives details of a similar custom at a spot in the River Boyne below Stackallen Bridge.

A deep pool immediately below the bridge receives the name of Log a' Ri, the King's Hole, where the river well deserves the name of 'the Broad Boyne' which it still retains. Some Ancient Pagan remembrances and superstitions attached to this locality up to a very recent date: and at a patron which used to be held here some years ago, it was customary for the people to swim their cattle across the river at this spot as a charm against fairies, and certain diseases as in former times they drove them though the Gap of Tara.

Many other such references can be found. In 1682, Sir Henry Piers in his description of Westmeath wrote:

On the first Sunday in harvest viz. in August they will be sure to drive their cattle into some pool or river and therein swim them: this they observe as inviolable as if it were a point of religion, for they think no beast will live the whole year thro' unless they be thus drenched: I deny not but that swimming of cattle, and chiefly in this season of the year is helthfull unto them . . . but precisely to do this on the first Sunday in harvest, I look on as not only superstitious but profane.

In 1838, O'Donovan mentioned a holy well called Tobar Alt an Easa, the Well of the Precipice of the Waterfall, in Kilmainham parish, Co. Meath, at which stations were performed on the first Sunday of each quarter. He went on to say that cattle were driven to this well 'from many parts of Cavan to be cured of their diseases', but gives no more details. This is St. Patrick's Well and it is still visited by pilgrims, but the custom of driving cattle to the well is no longer remembered locally.

Bishop Pocock in 1758 mentioned another method of keeping cattle healthy which was practiced at Loch Ine, a sea loch on the coast of West Cork. After a description of the loch, he went on:

there is a well for sprinkling the cows that have the murraine, and there is an altar at it where they say mass for them.

A striking example of this method of protecting the cattle was given by O'Donovan from Kilcummin parish, Co. Kerry. He wrote:

In the townland of Gortnagowan in the East division of this Parish there is a caher or circular stone fort called Caher-Crobhderg i.e. the fort of the Redhanded. In the west side of it is a holy well at which stations are performed by the peasentry on May Eve: who also drove their cattle into the fort and made them drink of the water of the holy well which is believed to have the virtue to preserve them from all contagious distempers during the ensuing year.

Such was the fame of Crobh Dearg that cattle were driven as much as 20–25 miles to get the benefit of her protection. According to the local story, Crobh Dearg (Red Claw) was one of three saintly sisters, of whom the other two were Gobnait and Latiaran. In this case, it is easy to see traces of the religion of the prechristian Irish. The story of a trio of saints, or women, or gods, or goddesses, comes from many parts of Ireland and was a notable feature of ancient Celtic religion. The date of this pilgrimage is also of significance because May Eve and May Day marked the beginning of summer and was certainly a major pagan festival, and a feature of this feast were measures to protect the cattle.

Another May Day practice to protect the cattle was described by Wilde:

When as a boy I used to visit on a May morning the great Rath at Crohan, near the rampart of which the cave's mouth (Hellmouth door of Ireland) is situated and when all the great Connaught oxen of the extensive plains around were driven in to be bled, and the peasantry gathered in with pots, turf, bags of meal, and bundles of scallions to make 'possets' with the warm blood as it flowed from the shoulders of the beeves.

Now, nearly a hundred and fifty years later, it is only possible to guess at the exact significance of this ritual. Bleeding was, and long continued to be, a standard method of treating animals, but it is clear that the time, May Day, and the place, the cave of Rathcroghan, take us back to a time long before Christianity. It may be that the cave was the entrance to the underworld of the Celtic gods who were believed to have lived in fairy mounds.

Perhaps the most dramatic description of all these strange survivals is described in the *Ordnance Survey Letters* from Co. Mayo (p. 368). O'Connor mentioned a small ruined church at Lough Ciaran in Bohola parish. He said:

At this lough which is a small pool in a bog to the left of the road leading by the old church of Bohola and nearly opposite the ruin there is usually a pattern held on the Sunday commonly called Garlick Sunday but recte Garland Sunday. . . . The people it is said swim their horses in the lake on that day to defend them against incidental evils during the year and throw spancels and halters into it which they leave there on the occasion. They are also accustomed to throw butter into it with the intention that their cows may be sufficiently productive of milk and butter during the year. The *clod ime* (lump of butter) thrown in at a time does not be more than a quarter of a pound weight. After the crowds have gone away, the poor who have not the necessaries of life otherwise than by obtaining them by alms from liberal or charitable persons, assemble and carry off as much of the butter as they can gather out of the lake. There was formerly a tree at this place around which the people were in the habit of fastening by a noose, cords (*buracha*) that were used in tying cows. The Roman Catholic bishop of the diocese in which the parish containing the old church and lough is situated, got the tree cut down in order to prevent the people from getting on with such ceremonies. The priests have dissuaded the people from getting on with their ceremonies at the lake so far that they are altogether giving them up. The stations are still practiced on the patron day, but the people are ceasing from throwing butter into it: or going on with their other practices at it.

Despite O'Connor's belief, the practice of throwing butter into the little lake was not given up at the time. I have been told that it was continued down to 1950 when traces of the butter could be seen floating on the surface. It may still be done, but at present it is not done openly.

The practice of swimming horses has been reported from a number of places. In Moylough parish, Co. Galway, there is a small lake called Loch Chill Eascrach. O'Donovan found that people used to swim horses in the lake 'to prevent accidents for the coming year'.

The practice of swimming horses is also reported from St. Ciaran's Well at Castlekeeran, Co. Meath, as well as from Lough Ciaran in Co. Mayo. The well is approached by an iron footbridge across a little stream, and was visited on the first Sunday in August. At that time it was the custom to ride horses through the stream. I visited the well on the 29th November 1975 and learned that the custom of swimming horses in the stream is no longer practiced. The reason why it was done was because the trickle from the holy well flowed into a little brook and made its water holy, so the horses were protected by the holy water of the brook.

This custom was mentioned in 1812 (E. Wakefield, *An Account of Ireland*) as being practiced in Co. Westmeath.

From Castletown Delvin to Lord Sunderlen's at Baronstown the people are all catholics and regular in attending places of worship. They are however much addicted to superstitious notions and make their horses swim in some of the lakes on Garlick Sunday, that is the second Sunday in August believing that this will render them healthy during the rest of the year.

This is also mentioned in a description of the pattern of Martry in Co. Meath.

But a custom with a distinct pagan touch was the swimming of horses in the river Blackwater before sunrise in the morning as a protection against disease. The horse carrying an almost naked rider was jumped or plunged into a deep pool in the river: it was necessary that the animal be completely wetted by the water.

SHEEP

The lake beside Loughrea in Co. Galway is mentioned in the *Dinshanchus*, which was written in the 10th century. It says that sheep were driven into the lake there and came out coloured red and it goes on to say that it was customary to drive the sheep of all Ireland every seven years into the lake.

I have not found any references to this being done in modern times.

XII

The Outsider at the Pattern

Visitors to this country during the eighteenth and nineteenth centuries often mentioned the patterns and in some cases they give very valuable information about them. Some of the visitors admired the laughter and high spirits of the crowds, but most of them violently disapproved of both the pilgrimages and the patterns. The Catholic Archbishop of Cashel was strongly against the custom of attending patterns and his words have been often quoted:

> It is become such a scene of drunkenness and quarrelling and of other most abominable vice, that religion herself is brought into disrepute nay mocked and ridiculed: intemperance and immorality are encouraged etc.

Shaw-Mason's *Parochial Survey* contains a number of references to patterns, most of them unfavourable. From Kilmactige parish, Co. Sligo, we get:

> A great number of saints' days are observed which however are spent in idleness and drinking to the great injury of the people both as to morals and industry.

Almost the same words were written from Kilgerriff in Co. Cork.

> Many holy days are kept on saints' days and Lady days, to the great prejudice of industry and the great emolument of ale houses.

The writer from St. Peter's parish, Athlone, mentioned three notable patterns in his neighbourhood, those at Brideswell, at St. John's Well, Lecarrow, and at Clonmacnoise. He said that three to four thousand people from all over Ireland attended the pattern at Clonmacnoise, which lasted for two days, and mentioned the 'drunken quarrels and obscenities' which took place there.

> At these places are always erected booths or tents as in fairs for

selling whiskey, beer and ale, at which pipers and fiddlers do not fail to attend, and the remainder of the day and night (after their religious performances are over and the priest withdrawn) is spent in singing, dancing and drinking to such excess that it seems more like the orgies of Baccus than the memory of a pious saint.

There is a similar description of a pattern at Tullaroan, Co. Kilkenny and the writer said that the pattern there sometimes continued for a week.

Some few favourable comments on the pilgrimages or patterns can be found in the *Parochial Survey*. From Fiddown parish in Co. Kilkenny, the writer said that formerly the crowd was well behaved but, 'now like a flock without a shepherd, the assemblies degenerate'. Large numbers of beggars attended the pattern at Lady's Island in Carne parish, Co. Wexford, and the writer described it as

the Lady's Island, a place of great devotion and pilgrimage as to the means in this parish of administering relief to the poor and wretched.

A pattern at the chapel of St. Eyen on the side of a hill over Loch Derravaragh in Co. Westmeath was described by Sir Henry Piers in 1682. After a description of the chapel, he continued:

To this chapel on the first Sunday in harvest, the natives pay their devotions in pilgrimages which for certain stages they undertake barefoot: but when they come to a certain noted place in the way they hold on the remainder of their devotion on their bare knees, all along to the chapel, on stone and gravel, intermixed and overgrown with heath and grass. Their devotion performed, they return merry and shod, no longer concerned for those sins that were the cause of this so severe a penance: but as if having now paid off the old score they longed to go on in the new again, they return in all haste to a green spot of ground on the east side of the hill, towards the land and here men and women fall a dancing and carousing the rest of the day: for ale sellers in great numbers on these days have their booth's here as in a fair and to be sure the merry bag-pipers fail not to pay their attendance. Thus in lewd and obscene dancing, and in excess of drinking the remainder of the day is spent as if they celebrated the Bacchanalia rather than the memory of a pious saint or their own penitentials: and often times it falls out that more blood is shed on the grass from broken pates and drunken quarrels when the pilgrimages are ended than was before on the stones from their bare feet and knees during their devotions.

The most striking description of a pattern was that written by Thackeray, in his *Irish Sketch Book* in 1842. He did not himself climb Cruach Patrick, but the practices were described to him.

The second station is on the top of the mountain. Here there is a great altar – a shapeless heap of stones. The poor wretches *crawl on their knees* into this place, say fifteen prayers, and after going round the entire top of the mountain fifteen times say fifteen prayers again.

The prayers mentioned appear to have been decades of the rosary and the fifteen would make a complete rosary. Thackeray went on:

My informant describes the people as coming away from this frightful exhibition suffering severe pain, wounded and bleeding in the knees and feet and some of the women shrieking with the pain of their wounds. Fancy thousands of these bent upon their work and priests standing by to encourage them! For shame. For shame . . . Of these tortures however I had not the fortune to witness a sight.

Later in the day, he travelled from Westport to the field at the foot of the mountain, where the pattern was going on despite the rain.

The pleasures of the poor people – for after the business on the mountain, came the dancing and love making at its foot – were woefully spoiled by the rain which rendered dancing on the grass impossible: nor were the tents big enough for that exercise. Indeed the whole sight was as dismal and half savage a one as I have seen. There may have been fifty of these tents squatted round a plain of the most brilliant green grass behind which the mist curtains seemed to rise immediately: for you could not even see the mountain-side beyond them. Here was a great crowd of men and women all ugly as the fortune of the day would have it (for the sagacious reader has no doubt remarked that there are ugly and pretty days in life). Stalls were spread about, whereof the owners were shrieking out the praises of their wares – great coarse damp looking bannocks of bread for the most part or mayhap a dirty collection of pigs-feet, and such refreshments. Several of the booths professed to belong to 'confectioners' from Westport or Castlebar, the confectionery consisting of huge biscuits and doubtful looking ginger beer – ginger ale or gingeretta it is called in this country by a fanciful people who love the finest titles. Add to these, cauldrons containing water for

Cruach Patrick, Co. Mayo. Pilgrims climbing the holy mountain.

'tay' at the door of the booths, other pots full of masses of pale legs of mutton (the owner 'prodding' every now and then for a bit and holding it up and asking the passenger to buy). In the booths, it was impossible to stand upright or to see much on account of the smoke. Men and women were crowded in these rude tents, huddled together and disappearing in the darkness. Owners came bustling out to replenish the emptied water jugs: and landladies stood outside in the rain calling strenuously upon all passers to enter.

Meanwhile, high up on the invisible mountain the people were dragging their bleeding knees from altar to altar, flinging stones and muttering some endless litanies with the priests standing by. I think I was not sorry that the rain, and the care of my precious health prevented me from mounting a severe hill to witness a sight that could only have caused one to be shocked and ashamed that servants of God should encourage it. The road home was very pleasant: everybody was wet through, but everybody was happy and by some miracle we were seven in the car.'

This description of the pattern at Cruach Patrick is the best one available. It will not need any explanation to those from rural Ireland who can remember the crowds and the discomfort of a wet day at a big sports day or football match, with the sellers of 'lemonade or lemon soda'. They will also recall the barrel of not very attractive-looking pigs' feet and 'standings' selling sweets and huge biscuits which Thackeray noticed. Some will remember the pots of boiling pieces of mutton, and these were seen at rural fairs in the west of Ireland up to the time of the second world war.

It will be realised that Thackeray was nearly an ideal witness. He was a brilliant writer, as well as being intelligent and friendly and did not have any more misapprehensions about the Irish than could reasonably be expected from a man of his time and class. Unfortunately he was too well fed, too well clothed, too well shod and too Protestant to understand the behaviour of people who had just climbed the Reek. Even more important, he was too much of a city man to enjoy what he would think of as a crude bucolic rural 'wake', and if he ever attended such a festival in the north of England, he might not understand it much better than he understood the doings at Cruach Patrick. Like so many others, he was horrified by the sight, or the thought, of barefoot pilgrims, and more so by the idea of pilgrims walking on their knees. No doubt his description of the priest supervising the rounds like someone presiding in a torture chamber must have caused suitable shudders of horror in London drawing-rooms. It is of interest that he does not mention any people who sold alcohol: no doubt Father Matthew had been to Co. Mayo by 1842.

There is a detailed description, written about thirty years later, of the pilgrimage and pattern at Glendalough in Co. Wicklow. The writer, Sir William Wilde, might be thought of as an expert on such patterns; he had been in the habit of attending them since his boyhood. He visited Glendalough on the eve of the pattern, the 3rd of June, and wrote:

> For many years I was in the habit of visiting 'the Churches,' on the eve of the Pattern or Patron Saint's Day and remaining until the faction fights, . . . The scene was remarkable and I and my friends often spent a large portion of the night walking among the ruins where an immense crowd usually had bivouacked or were putting up tents and booths or cooking their evening meal, gypsy-wise, throughout the space of the sacred enclosure. As soon as daylight dawned, the tumbling torrent over the rocks and stones of the Glendassan river to the north of 'the Churches' became crowded with penitents wading, walking, and kneeing up to St. Kevin's Keeve, many of them holding little children in their

Glendalough, Co. Wicklow. The "Seven Churches".

arms. 'The Deer Stone' was visited by strangers and pilgrims and always found to contain water! The guides arranged the penitential routes, or conducted tourists round the ruins with the usual forms of expression used by their class. Dancing, drinking, thimble-rigging, prick-o-the-loop, and other amusements, even while the bareheaded venerable pilgrims and bare kneed Voteens were going their prescribed rounds, continued. Towards evening the fun became 'fast and furious,' the pilgrimages ceased, the dancing was arrested, the pipers and fiddlers escaped to places of security, the keepers of tents and booths looked to their gear, the crowd thickened, the brandishing of sticks, the 'hoshings' and 'wheelings' and 'hieings' for their respective parties showed that the faction fight was about to commence among the tombstones and monuments and that all the religious observances and even refreshments were at an end. Police and magistrates were often required. What a change has taken place during the past twenty years. The present worthy parish priest on pattern days some twenty years ago, collected the sticks of the combatants, and by his mild but determined influence assuaged the angry feelings aroused simply by the contiguity of the combatants. The Patron Saint's Day at Glendalough on 3rd June is no longer celebrated.

Wilde was certainly a friendly witness and an exact one and he was long familiar with, and probably enjoyed, the fun as much as any of the crowd.

The customs at patterns generally were described by Piers in his *Description of Westmeath*. He wrote in 1682:

> On the patron day in most parishes as also on the feasts of Easter and Whitsuntide the more ordinary sort of people meet near the ale house in the afternoon on some convenient spot of ground and dance for the cake: here to be sure the piper fails not of diligent attendance. The cake to be danced for is provided at the charge of the alewife and is advanced on a board on the top of a pike about ten feet high: this board is round and from it riseth a kind of garland beset and tied round with meadow flowers if it be early in the summer, if later the garland the addition of apples set round on pegs fastened onto it: the whole number of dancers begin all at once in a large ring a man and a woman and dance round about the bush, so is the garland called, and the piper as long as they are able to hold out: they that hold out longest at the exercise win the cake and apples and then the ale-wife's trade goes on.

It will be seen from these descriptions that the pattern was just like any rural summer festival, at any time, or in any place. There was the usual eating, drinking, courting, loud talk and laughter, which could be expected at such a place and the opposition to the patterns appears to have been a reflection of the respectability of the Victorian age. At that time, 'progress' was the great ideal with steamships and railways leading the way to a bright happy future when God would be sure to help those who helped themselves. A liberal evangelical Protestant might tolerate the pattern as to be expected from those who still sat in darkness, but he could not tolerate the practice of doing pilgrimages to holy wells or the practice of walking barefoot round stones, trees and such things. The fact that the parish priest often encouraged the people to visit the holy wells would seem to be no better than gross superstition.

It would be expected that there would be some fighting on pattern days, and there is plenty of evidence of this. Faction fighting with the blackthorn sticks was common at fairs and such places during the first half of the nineteenth century in all parts of Ireland. It was rough and sometimes dangerous and the authorities were inclined to regard it as a danger to the public peace, and their efforts to stop it often caused more trouble than a faction fight; but organised faction fighting at patterns does not appear to have been common: the only certain example is Wilde's description of the fighting at Glendalough. As has been seen, there are many unfavourable references to patterns in Shaw-Mason's *Parochial Survey*. These were written by ministers of the Established Church who would normally be opposed to the practice of such things as visiting holy wells, and this would colour their description of them. Even if they are known to be hostile witnesses, they often provide useful information.

It will be realised therefore that almost all the evidence cited in this chapter is given by hostile witnesses. Nevertheless it is clear that patterns were ordinary rural festivals and the behaviour of the crowd was exactly what could be expected at such gatherings.

XIII

Pilgrimages to Holy Islands

It will be noticed that ruins of ancient churches and early monastic settlements are found on many islands off the Irish coast and also on the islands in Irish lakes. It is not clear why this became the practice in the early Irish church: it may have been for security or in an effort to avoid contact with the outside world, but there may have been other reasons why the Irish monks sought out such places. Some of these islands may have been holy places before the arrival of Christianity, and the Christian missionaries replaced the druids.

It would be quite impossible to examine all the holy islands of Ireland in a book of this kind, so only a few of the more notable islands will be mentioned. The selection is almost unlimited and it is difficult to see why some islands were thought holy and others not. Pilgrimages to the more accessible islands were carried out at fixed times in the usual way, but in some cases there was no fixed time and pilgrims went to the holy islands when the sea was calm enough to make the crossing. A pilgrimage to one of these remote places was most often undertaken voluntarily, or in fulfilment of a promise made in time of trouble, but in some cases it might be imposed by a confessor on a penitent. The pilgrims usually travelled barefoot, and in groups, taking a number of days on the journey, and probably they enjoyed the trip in good summer weather. Today most pilgrims to Lourdes or Rome enjoy the new experience as a change from their routine lives and no doubt the pilgrims to Scellig, or to Inishmurray had many stories to tell when they got home. As a child, I remember seeing a barefoot pilgrim walking to the holy island in Loch Derg, Co. Donegal.

INISHMURRAY

Most of these holy islands are treasure houses for the archaeologist and of them all Inishmurray has been the most completely described. It is a flattened oval containing 200 acres, about a mile from east to west, and is about 4½ miles from the nearest point of the mainland. Rats are not found there and mice only came to the island recently as punishment for the killing of someone's cow. The most prominent feature is the *caiseal* built of dry stone work, roughly pear shaped with its longest diameter 175 feet. Inside the *caiseal* are the remains of three churches, Teach Molaise, Teampull na bhFear, and Teampull na Teinidh, as well as a number of *Clochans*.

There was no fixed date or season at which the pilgrims came, due to the difficulty of reaching the island in currachs. The pilgrims first prayed at Teach Molaise, where the people of the island used gather for prayers on Sunday. From Teach Molaise the pilgrims moved clockwise around the island pausing to pray at ten stations (*leachta*) on the journey. These stations were all built on the same pattern. They each consisted of uncemented stones set together in the form of a cube about five feet square and four feet high with a cross incised slab raised in the centre of the cube. This 'altar' was surrounded by a low dry stone wall rarely more than 2 – 3 feet high. On the circuit of the island the stations were called, in order, Olla Muire, Trath-na-righ fhear, Leachta Crois Mor, Tratan Aodha, and Leachta Phadruig, at the most easterly point of the island. From there the pilgrims went to Trionid Mor, Trionid Beg, Leachta Choluim-Chille and Reilic Odrain. In addition, there were three 'altars' inside the *caiseal*, an Altoir Beg, the Eastern Altar and, most notable of all, one called the Clocha-breacha, which had a large number of rounded stones on the top and was said to have been a cursing altar (See pp. 83, 111 for illustrations).

The ritual carried out at each station is not described, but it is likely that the pilgrims first moved clockwise round each altar outside the little wall, saying a few simple prayers. Then they may have gone inside and prayed at the altar before moving round it inside the wall. Near an entrance to the *caiseal*, is Tobar Molaise, covered by a round, beehive shaped covering called a *clochan*. The pilgrim ended by praying at this well and drinking some of the water which Wakeman said was neither abundant nor palatable.

In addition to Tobar Molaise, there are two other holy wells on the island, Tobar na Suil and Tobar na Coragh (Well of Assistance). Tobar na Coragh contains bright, clear water and a stream from it runs through a stone lined channel, which may have been used as a bath, into the sea. Wakeman was told of a custom of drawing this well to calm the sea, in bad weather, when the island had been storm bound, but he could not learn when this had last been done. People were reluctant to speak of this practice.

There are many features of interest in the island, all of which were described by Wakeman in his splendid monograph. These included Teach-na-Teinidh on the floor of which a perpetual fire burned. A visitor to the island, a Scotsman, heard of the fire and went to see it. With a sense of black humour he micturated on it, and to his surprise it suddenly blazed up fiercely, and the man was burned to death. Wakeman said that in a niche in the east wall there were some partly burned human bones (p.144). The men of the island were buried at Teampull na bhFear, inside the *caiseal*, while the women were buried at Teampull na mBan outside it. It was believed that if a woman was buried at Teampull na bhFear, the body would move during the night to Teampull na mBan and similarly the body of a man would move to Teampull na bhFear.

INIS GLUAIRE

This island off the coast of the Mullet peninsula in Co. Mayo, contains 37 acres and is shaped like a rough figure of eight, lying north-west and south-east, with most of the ruined buildings at the south-east end. In was believed to be the holiest island in the neighbourhood and has been famous for hundreds of years. Geraldus Cambrensis wrote in the twelfth century:

There is an island called Aren (?) situated in the western part of Connaught and consecrated to St. Brendan where human corpses are neither buried or decay, but deposited in the open air remain uncorrupted ... There is another thing remarkable in this island. Although mice swarm in vast numbers in other parts of Ireland here not a single one is found. No mouse is bred here nor does it live if it be introduced: when brought over it runs immediately away and leaps into the sea. If it be stopped it immediately dies.

Some centuries later this was written in the *Book of Ballymote*:

On Inis Gluair in Irrus Donnan the bodies thither brought do not rot but their nails and hair grow and everyone there recognises his father and grandfather for a long time after death: and no meat whatever will putrify on it even without being salted.

This story is only a little less wonderful than that of the island where nobody could die, and it is taken as proof of the great sanctity of the place, and the absence of mice there is a further proof of this unusual sanctity.

Inishmurray. The wall ambry in Teach na Teinidh (The House of the Fire). Some fragments of burned human bones are kept in it. *See p. 143.*

The buildings on Inis Gluaire resemble those found on Inish-murray. There are two ruined churches, one known as Teampull na bhFear or Teampull na Naomh, and the other slightly smaller is Teampull na mBan. The chapel of St. Brendan is very small, 12 feet × 8 feet, and built of dry stone, with the remains of a corbelled roof. Part of the wall of the caiseal remains. It appears to have been much less strong and elaborate than that on Inishmurray. The seven *Leachta* are in two groups. Four are found at the north-west end of the island, and three at the south-east end, close to the other buildings. There is also a pillar stone nine feet tall with a heap of small stones at its base and another large stone called Cloch na h-Athchuinge (The Stone of the Petitions) on the top of which O'Donovan saw two small heaps of stones. The holy well dedicated to St. Brendan is covered by a clochan called *tor tiprait* (Tower of the well) and is approached by an uncovered passage 9 feet long and down seven steps. It is a very special well and no woman may draw water from it.

In doing the pilgrimage it is the custom to go round each *leachta* three times on the knees and then three times walking and saying seven Paters, seven Aves and a Creed, in honour of God and St. Brendan. The first leachta is called Leachta Reilig Muire. The pilgrims end at Cloch na h-Athcunga, where they say seven Paters, seven Aves and a Creed and might then ask God for some favour. A small man-made cave, called *An Uaigh*, was probably visited by the pilgrims and they may have kept a vigil in it.

When O'Donovan visited the island there was a wooden statue of St. Brendan there to which wonderful powers were attributed, but this has now disappeared. Among the many legends which have been told about Inis Gluaire, the best known is the story of the Children of Lir who were buried there by St. Brendan, when they finally died after living as enchanted swans for nine hundred years. There is also the story of a causeway leading from the island to the old church of Kilmore on the mainland. It was also the practice that when a ship sailed close to the island, the crew lowered the topsail in honour of St. Brendan.

Two other holy islands off the coast of Galway may be mentioned briefly. These are Inishark, where St. Leo is honoured, and St. Mac Dara's Island. On Inishark there are the saint's church, his bed, his cross and a clochán. There are fourteen praying stations on the island and the pilgrims ended by praying at the well and sleeping at the clochan. St. Mac Dara's Island is only visited on the saint's feast days, 16th July and 28th September, when the holy well is usually found dry. A wooden statue was also preserved here until as Rory

O'Flaherty recorded, 'Malachias Queleus the Archbishop of Tuam caused it to be buried underground for special weighty reasons.' It was also the custom that ships sailing between the island and Mason Head dipped their sails in honour of St. Mac Dara and there was a story of the harm which befell two men who did not do this. It was also the custom to name boats Mac Dara in order to ensure their safety.

CAHER ISLAND (CAHER PHADRUIG)

This island of 128 acres is a rough oval and lies between Clare Island and Inish Boffin off the coast of Co. Mayo. The long axis of the oval runs nearly north west and south east. Near the north-west end of the island is a holy well called Tobar Muire, which is held in great veneration by the pilgrims. The ancient church, Teampull Phadruig, with its small graveyard and some other artefacts are near the south-east end. Near the church six leachta are shown on the Ordnance Map, but O'Donovan's informants could not, or perhaps would not, tell him their names. East of the east gable of the church there is a cross inscribed flagstone called Leabaidh Phadruig, which the pilgrims also visit, and O'Donovan recorded the words of a prayer which they said:

> Mo Leabidh is cearchuil chruaidhe
> Mairg a Christ a chuaidh na seilbh.
> (My bed and hard ring. Pity O Christ who went to death).

This island is a very holy place, being ranked next to Inis Gluaire in order of sanctity. As usual, no rats live on the island and clay from it will destroy rats or mice anywhere. It was also believed that anyone suffering from epilepsy would be cured if he slept for a few minutes in Teampull Phadruig or on Leabaidh Phadruig or even anywhere on the island. Near the south-east end at the water's edge is a structure called Boher na Niamh, which was believed to be the remains of the road taken by St. Patrick, St. Brigid and the rest of the halo of saints who went with them from Caher Island to Cruach Patrick. Another custom was that boatmen as they sailed past the island took off their caps and prayed:

> Umh luighmid do Dhia Mhor na n-uile
> Chumhachta agus do Phadruig Miorbhuilteach.
> (We submit to the Great God of all Power and to Patrick the miracle worker).

The island was famous, or infamous, for its cursing stone called Leac na Naomh, which O'Donovan saw on the altar of Teampull Phadruig. This has been described elsewhere in the book.

SCEILLIG MHICHIL

This rock, which covers 44 acres, must be one of the most inaccessible holy islands in the world. It is dedicated to St. Michael, the Archangel, and may be compared to similar 'high places', one in Cornwall and the other in Normandy, where St. Michael is also honoured. It is little more than a barren rock, nine miles off the coast of Kerry, rising very steeply from the sea, and it is only possible to land on it in very calm weather. The most detailed description is by Charles Smith, in his *History of Kerry*, published in 1756. He began by saying that it was a 'stupendious rock which was until these few years past visited by great numbers of people ever since the time of St. Patrick, says Keating, by way of piety and devotion.' He continued:

> Here are several stone crosses erected, at which the pilgrims perform certain stationary prayers and have peculiar orizons to perform at each station. When they have visited the cells and chapels they ascend the top of the rock, part of which is performed by squeezing through a hollow part resembling the funnel or shaft of a chimney which they term 'the Needle's Eye'. This ascent (altho there are holes and steps cut into the rock to climb by,) is far from being gained without trouble: but when this obstacle is surmounted the pilgrim arrives at a small flat place about a yard broad which slopes away down both sides of the rock to the ocean: on the further side of this flat which from its narrowness on the top is a kind of isthmus the ascent is gained by climbing up a smooth sloping rock that only leans out a very little, and this they call 'the Stone of Pain' from the difficulty of its ascent: there are a few shallow holes cut in it where they fix their hands and feet and by which they scramble up. This kind of a sloping wall is about twelve feet high and the danger of mounting it seems terrible for if a person should slip, he might tumble on either side down a precipice headlong, many fathoms into the sea. With this difficult passage the remaining part of the way up to the highest summit of the rock is much less difficult. On the top are two stations to visit where there are also some stone crosses: the first is called 'the Eagle's Nest' . . . The second station which the devotees have to visit on this height and which is attended with the utmost horror and peril is by some called 'the Spindle'

147

Sceillig Mhichil. Clocháns and part of the cashel. See p. 147.

See p. 147.

and others 'the Spit', which is a long narrow fragment of rock
projecting from the summit of this frightful place over a raging
sea: and this is walked to by a narrow path of only two feet in
breadth and several steps in length. Here the devotees, women as
well as men, sit astride on this rock and so edge forward until they
arrive at a stonecross which some bold adventurer cut formerly
on its extreme end: and having repeated a Pater Noster, returning from thence concludes the penance. To get back down 'the
Stone of Pain' is attended with some Address in order to land
safe on the neck of rock which I called an isthmus.

There are surprisingly extensive remains of buildings on the rock. These consist of a small church dedicated to St. Michael, and three small oratories. There are also six *clochans*, a *caiseal* and numerous crosses and cross incised slabs. It has been a place of pilgrimage since the beginning of Christianity in Ireland and nowadays some people still go to Sceillig Mhichil to pray in the holy place, even though there are no regular pilgrimages to it.

INIS CEALTRA

This island, is near Scarrif in Loch Derg, the largest of the Shannon lakes. Until about 150 years ago a pilgrimage, which began on the Friday before Whitsunday and continued for four days, was famous and attended by large crowds, but only the most vague memory of this remains. Luckily, John O'Donovan was able to record a description of it, and to this Philip Dixon Hardy's description may be added. O'Donovan heard that:

> The station was commenced at Lady Well and the performers went round the extremity of the island, one mile in circuit, seven

Two typical praying stations with the peaks of Cruach Patrick in the distance.

149

times = seven miles. The short rounds were commenced at a
station monument (a little mound of earth and stones) lying 35
yards to the west of the round tower. They went round this
monument seven times and proceeded through the door in the
west gable of St. Caimin's Church and as far as the altar in St.
Columb's Chapel. They went this length seven times from the
monument just mentioned, and at the commencement of every
seven of these, they went round the monument itself seven times.
They went round St. Caimin's Church fourteen times, the tower
and all the churches being included in the rounds. They went
round a station monument at the end of St. Caimin's Church . . .
They also went seven times round St. Michael's Garden and
seven times round the bank of earth about St. Michael's Church,
and seven times round the church itself, and seven times round a
large flagstone lying at it on which stone they finally (i.e. having
gone round it seven times) impressed kisses. They went seven
times round St. Mary's Church and seven times round the Baptismal Church. They finished at the well and drank its water.

This is not a very clear description of the pilgrimage, and it would
seem that O'Donovan's informant did not remember the exact
ritual.

Dixon Hardy quoting 'an Eye Witness' began by mentioning
some of the legends of the island, such as the story that all the
buildings were built in one night, and that the round tower would
have been built up to heaven if some woman had not asked the saint
'How high do you intend to build it?' There was also a legend that
Our Lady came to meet St. Patrick on Inis Cealtra.

He then went on to give a long description of the pilgrimage and
he wrote at length and with horror of all the penitential exercises.

All of them are considered trifling in comparison to the last for
this is performed on the naked knees through a heap of rugged
stones: the females tuck up their clothes and expose their persons
in the most indelicate manner. Men of the most dissolute morals
go to witness this part of the exhibition but none can witness the
finale without feelings of the greatest horror being excited: when
it comes to this all must (without assistance) descend on the
naked knees a step nearly a foot in depth. This is a most painful
operation.

Two pages later he continued:

You generally find all the abandoned females of the country.
When the penance is finished the grossness of the language is

most disgusting . . . When the work of penance is finished all repair to the tents, the drinking then commences and in the evening the island is more like the ancient Cyprus when dedicated to Venus, than a place to which the frequenters of it ascribe holiness. It is polluted with drunken revels and the most gross debauchery.

O'Donovan went on to explain why the pattern had been stopped: the local squireens would steal the girls at it. He wrote:

Three brothers of a family of the O'Briens who resided in the county of Clare within view of the island used to frequent the patron, at which they conducted themselves in a most disgraceful manner. On one occasion, one of them carried off a young girl by force from it: whom he afterwards detained till he had three children by her.

One could agree that respectable Victorian ladies and gentlemen would be shocked at the doings of the crowd at the pattern. Hardy and his authority, the Reverend James Page, knew that it was all due to the evil influence of Popery, and they must have been greatly troubled by the sight of all the cheerful sinners hurrying along the road to hell. Following some recent excavations on Inis Cealtra, the pilgrimage has been re-established.

INIS CAOL

This is a tidal island of 80 acres, on the south shore of Gweebarra Bay in Co. Donegal. It is dedicated to St. Conall Caol and was visited between 22nd May and 12th of September, when the pilgrims visit St. Conall's Well, and a well dedicated to the Blessed Virgin.

O'Donovan visited the island and was not impressed:

On this island the natives were in the habit of performing *turases* i.e. tours or pilgrimages but latterly it becomes a place of amusement and drinking so that the R.C. clergy thought it proper to condemn the practice, to the rapid decrease in the fame of Conall the Slender.

During the *turas* the senior of the house of O'Breslin (of which family St. Conall is said to have been a member and the patron) attended with the bell of the saint called Bearnan Conall. He generally sat or stood or knelt at a sacred rocky place called Conall's Bed and praying in Latin held forth the bell to be kissed by the pilgrims for which office it was a part of the ceremony that he should receive more or less from each of them.

Despite this the pilgrimage is still a popular one and a leaflet written by Father Charles Boyce, the parish priest, gives details of the ritual followed today. The pilgrim first prays at St. Conall's Well and then at the saint's Bed. From there he goes to and walks round three piles of stones, one after the other, and then goes to the well dedicated to Our Lady. The next station is a large stone behind the churchyard and he makes three circuits of the stone. Next he makes a circuit of St. Conall's Church and finishes his prayers kneeling at the altar in the church. Then kneeling and looking out through the church door he offers prayers in honour of St. Conall and St. Dallan, and to get the benefits of the pilgrimage. A note at the end of the leaflet reads: 'N.B. No Money Offering to be left on the Island.'

An unusual *turas* which was done by pilgrims to Inis Caol was described by P.J. MacGill in his book on Ardara parish. In this case, the pilgrims started from the holy island and followed a route laid out by St. Conall. They went first to Oiter Chonaill on Carn Strand. From there to St. Conall's Cross and from there to St. Conall's Well on the peninsula of Loughross and then across another bay, Loughross Beg Bay to a cross incised stone at Laconnell and from there back to Inis Caol. This journey across two bays would be at least twenty miles. I do not know if any pilgrims do this long *turas* nowadays, but on a long pleasant summer day, it could be a pleasant walk, and one does not imagine a crowd of lads and lassies walking gravely and saying a succession of rosaries. Most of them had relatives and friends along the way and would probably visit them and remain overnight.

INIS CATHAIGH

This holy island contains 180 acres and lies in the estuary of the Shannon, two miles south of Kilrush Quay in Co. Clare. It has all the usual legends. St. Senan attacked and expelled an evil beast called 'the Cathach' from his island. He built seven churches there, floated across the Shannon on a stone, and like some other Irish saints, did not want any women on his island.

Shaw Mason said that the people of the neighbourhood wished to bury their dead in the island, but this was not always possible in stormy weather. In such a case a burial place called Shanakill was used and people believed that all the bodies buried in Shanakill were moved miraculously under the bed of the river into the holy island. T.A. Westropp described an inscribed stone which was in the garden of a house called Nabocleish Cottage, near Kilkee. The inscription in very rough verse was copied by John Windle and is clearly a description of the pilgrimage. It reads:

In the name of God Amen.
Bare head, bare feet, all pious Christians are to kneel
At every station say or read 5 Paters Aves and a Creed
5 times round each blessed place
Singing hymns and partner beads (Paidrín Páirteach)
Round the altar is a first
And 2 noted stations on the strand annex
Round the island at water edge: 4th the Nun's toomb on the strand due West
Whoever kneels and reads a prayer will not meet a watery grave
Bring up a stone to monument hill perform there and that's the 5th
6th N-East a place called Laoth (Leacht) and at Our Lady's Church women stop
8th the large church. 9th is the Srs (?Saviour's).
10th is the bed called St. Synan's Grave. The well is 11th finish and pray for ye souls of ye Erectors of this Blessed Place.

On the other side of the stone the Crucifixion was carved with a round tower, an angel, a figure holding a chalice and 'St. Synan with a crosier driving out a beast serrated back belly and tail.' Windle showed a somewhat fish shaped spikey monster with two three toed fore-feet, and upcurled nose and small mouth, the famous 'Cata' which Senan expelled from the island.

About the year 1800, the parish priest wished to discourage people from going to Inis Cathaigh, so he had the stone removed to the mainland. There was also the story of a curate who, about the year 1827 persuaded some of the women of the island to enter St. Senan's Church. Within a short time, they and their families were evicted and were forced to leave the island.

LADY'S ISLAND

This holy island, joined to the mainland by a causeway, is found in a tidal lake, a few miles west of Carnsore Point, on the south coast of Wexford. It contains 32 acres and on it are the ruins of a castle which was built to defend the causeway, as well as the ruins of a small church and an ancient graveyard.

In 1840, John O'Donovan wrote that Irish speakers from

153

Kilkenny used to refer to the island as Oilean Muire. Although the pilgrimage had been discontinued in his time, he said that forty years before it had been as popular as the pilgrimage to the holy island in Loch Derg, Co. Donegal. He suggested that, originally, the patron may have been St. Barry, but the early English and Norman settlers who knew little of St. Barry, knew much more about the Virgin Mary and may have made the change. The church ruins are not more than a few centuries old.

About the year 1680, the pilgrimage was described by a friendly witness who knew all about it. Two years later, a much more detailed description was written by a very hostile witness, Col. Solomon Richards, one of the new Cromwellian landowners. Both descriptions have been published in *JRSAI* Col. Richards wrote:

> In this lough is an island called Lady's Island, in former times of Ignorance highly esteemed and accounted Holy – and to this day the natives, persons of honour as well as others, in aboundance from remote parts of the Kingdom doe with great devotion go on pilgrimage thither, and there doe penance going bare-leg and bare-foote, dabling in the water up to mid leg round the Island. Some others goe one foote in the water, the other on dry land taking care not to wet the one, nor to tread dry with the other. But some great sinners goe on their knees in the water round the island and some others that are greater sinners yet goe three times round on their knees in the water. This I have seen, as also I have seen persons of no mean degree leave their hose and shoes in Wexford and goe bare-footed in dirty weather from Wexford to this Island which is eight miles and having done their penance made their offering in the chapell and return to Wexford in the same posture. This aboundance of people (not the wisest) doe every year towards the end of summer – but the chiefest or most meritorious time is betwixt their two Lady days of August 15 and September 8. If any Lady through indisposition be loath to wet her feete, there are women allowed to do it for them, they being present and paying half a crown for a fee. . . . And this pennance is effective enuffe.

The unknown friendly witness gives less detail but is full of enthusiasm for the pilgrimage. He wrote:

> Within this Ismus is a church builded and dedicated to the glorious and imaculate Virgin Mother by impotent and infirme pilgrims, and a multitude of persons of all qualityes from all provinces and parts of Ireland daily frequented and with fervent

devotion visited who, praying and making several oblacions or extending charitable Benevolence to Indigents there residing, having been miraculously cured of grievous Maladies and helped to the perfect use of naturally defective Limmes, or accidentally enfeebled or impaired Senses.

In this century, the pilgrimage has again become very popular, and the season still extends from August 15 to September 8. On 15 August this year (1978) nearly 20,000 people visited the island, according to a newspaper report and as the report says:

One of the most remarkable aspects of Our Lady's Island is the complete lack of commercialism associated with the pilgrimage.

The pilgrims still move round the island at the water's edge but I did not learn of any of them who now do it barefoot. It is of course greatly favoured by the Church and the pilgrim prayers are recited aloud by the pilgrims, with the aid of an efficient public address system and a number of well placed loud-speakers.

XIV

The Future

While this book was being written people pointed out to me that many holy wells which had once been visited by large numbers of pilgrims were no longer visited and would soon be forgotten. Sometimes they would add, in case I should feel hurt by what they had said, that it was great to have a book written on the subject while the custom still survived. At first look these people would appear to be right. Fewer people now visit their local holy wells and I do not know of anything resembling a nineteenth century pattern which has continued until the present day. I know that people still visit and pray at holy wells for a cure of some ailments, but now it is much more likely that a mother would take her sick baby to the Child Welfare Clinic than to a holy well. Surely everyone will agree that this is a change for the better. These days crowds are more likely to gather to see a pop star or to hear a punk rock group where they can enjoy themselves shouting as well as fighting and getting drunk. This again is better than drinking and faction fighting at a pattern.

During the last century the pattern day was a public holiday and people visited the holy well as part of the holiday. Then all the pilgrims walked – they had no other ways of travelling – and consequently the pattern was a very local affair. Few people then went far from their native district.

Now in the second half of the twentieth century travel has become cheaper and easier, and people travel more than they have ever done. In addition, with the aid of television we come to feel that we can see history being made, and in the course of a week it is possible to see more countries than a mediaeval traveller would see in a lifetime, all without leaving the armchair.

These two developments, cheap comfortable travel and television, have led to a decline in people's interest in their local activities, such as the local sports day or the race meeting, and also the pattern at the local holy well.

The Future

Pilgrims have always managed to convert a pilgrimage into a holiday outing. Anyone who has ever travelled with a group of pilgrims will know this, and now thousands of them travel to such places as Lourdes, Fatima and Rome. In this way they enjoy a continental holiday as well as a pilgrimage and this has led to a further decline in the numbers of people visiting the local holy well. There is little doubt that this will continue as more and more people travel to the continent.

While this is so, it is also apparent that easy travel and television have made many pilgrimages better known. More people than ever visit such famous places as Lady's Island in Wexford and Tobar an Ailt near Sligo, and the barefoot pilgrims have been seen on the television climbing Croagh Patrick.

At present the most popular place of pilgrimage is the small village called Knock in Co. Mayo. It is believed that in the year 1879 the Blessed Virgin appeared there to some of the people of the village and since then increasing numbers of pilgrims have gone there. Over the years a great church has been built on the spot to accommodate the very large crowds and there must be few parishes in Ireland from which at least one group of pilgrims does not travel to Knock every year.

In September 1979 many of the television screens of the world showed Pope John Paul II when he visited the village and on that day more than a quarter of a million people were there to see him and to pray. Here are all the trappings of a popular pilgrimage, processions, shops selling the souvenirs which pilgrims buy, and hundreds of invalids. A medical bureau has been established to care for these, and to investigate scientifically any cures which may be claimed. Lately, plans for an airport and a large hotel are being considered.

The best known of all the holy island pilgrimages is surely that to Station Island in Loch Derg, Co. Donegal, which continues from June 1 to August 15. This small island with its great church, and hostels where the pilgrims live, is startling as it is seen rising from the peat brown water of the lake. The hills around the lake are covered with bare moorland and the only activity to be seen from the holy island is the arrival of cars and buses with pilgrims from all parts of the northern half of Ireland.

When one reaches the island it is even more surprising to see the hundreds of barefoot pilgrims doing the rounds of the 'beds', each one busy saying the prescribed prayers. I recall feeling, as I went the rounds, that it would be great if I could get a pair of socks and shoes to protect my feet which were cold and painful. On the day they

157

arrive the pilgrims do the station rounds twice, and then they have their one meal of dry bread and black tea. After that, if you are thirsty you drink water to which you may add salt, making it 'wine' as the pilgrims say. The night is spent keeping vigil in the church, during which the station prayers are said three times. At last the summer night is over and the tired pilgrims attend Mass and listen to a long sermon. After a day of quiet and rest and another meal of dry bread and black tea the pilgrims may go to bed, but not before 8.00 p.m. Next morning, after Mass and another round of the stations, the pilgrims leave the island and have their third meal of dry bread when they reach home.

This pilgrimage, which is unique in the Latin Church will certainly never decline. There are no votive offerings on the island, no miraculous cures are claimed, and there is nothing of power or glory to be seen. It is a very ancient pilgrimage and in doing it one is back in the ancient Celtic church. So far I have not heard of a television programme on the Loch Derg pilgrimage.

During the twentieth century the importance of the local holy well may further decline, as increasingly larger crowds visit the more famous places. In this they will show that the practice is vigorously alive and able to adapt to the present time. It is not the pious who go to these places. It is, as it always was, the ordinary people, for religion as distinct from piety is one of the great driving forces of the human race.

Glossary of Irish Words

aingeal	an angel
ált	a cliff face, a steep side of a valley
árd	high, a height, ard
bachall	a shepherd's crook, a crozier
baile	a homestead, a town, *bally*
bean	a woman
bilé	a sacred historic tree
bó	a cow
bóthar	a road, *boher*
breac	speckled
buarach	a spancel
bullán	a rounded hollow in a stone, man made, probably a primitive food mixer
caiseal	a stone fort, an enclosing wall, *cashel*
carraig	a rock, *carrack*
ceallúin	a churchyard, the area around a ruined church
cill	a church, *kill*
cillín	area of churchyard used to bury unbaptised infants, probably the site of a forgotten church
cloch	a stone
clochán	a small round building built of dry stone with a corbelled roof
clod	a lump
cnoc	a hill, *knock*
cos	a foot
craobh	a branch, a tree
cuaille	a club, a walking stick, a special tree
dabhach	a vat, a large vessel, a well
dorcha	dark
drom	the back, a ridge of land, *drum*
eas	a waterfall, a cataract

159

fear	a man
fionn	fair-haired, white, beautiful
gamhain	a calf
gealt	a lunatic
im	butter
inis	an island, a peninsula, *ennis, inish*
leac	a flagstone
leacht	a grave, a cairn, a monument
mám	a mountain pass
molt	a wether
mór	great, large
Muire	The Virgin Mary
ogham	an early form of writing
oileán	an island
oll	great, used in compound words, i.e. *oll-phiart*, a great serpent
poll	a hole
sídh	a fairy hill, *shee*
sliabh	a mountain, *slieve*
sneacht	snow
súil	an eye
teach	a house, a church
teampall	a church, *temple*
teine	a fire
tobar	a well, *tubber*
turas	a journey, pilgrimage
turlach	a winter lake, dried up in the summer
uaigh	a grave, den, cave

Principal Authorities and Sources Cited

1. Adomnan. *Life of Columba*. Ed. Anderson and Anderson 1961.
2. Bonner B. *Culdaff and Cloncha*. DA 1970.
3. Cordner W.S. 'Some Old Wells in Antrim and Down'. *UJA* Vol 3 et vol 5.
4. Cordner W.S. 'The Cult of the Holy Well'. *UJA* Vol. 9.
5. Crawford H. 'Holy Well near Ballinskelligs' et ff *JRSAI* Vol. 45 (c).
6. Danaher K. 'The Holy Wells of Co. Dublin'. *Archiv. Hib*. Vol. 2.
7. Danaher K. 'The Holy Wells of Co. Limerick'. *JRSAI* 1955.
8. Danaher K. 'The Holy Wells of Corcaguinny' *JRSAI* 1960.
9. Dillon M. and Chadwick N. *The Celtic Realms* 2nd edition.
10. Dublin Holy Wells Records in Ordnance Survey Office. Archeology Section.
11. Frazer W. ' "Holed" and Perforated Stones' *JRSAI* Vol. 26.
12. Fitzergerald E. 'Ardmore'. *JRSAI* Vol. 4.
13. Fitzgerald W. 'Father Moore's Well'. *JCKAS* 1918.
14. Fitzgerald W. 'The Holed Stone of Castledermot' *JRSAI* Vol. 22.
15. Geraldus Cambrensis. *The Topography of Ireland*. Ed. Wright 1905.
16. Hardy P.D. *The Holy Wells of Ireland*. 1836.
17. Hartnett J.P. 'The Holy Wells of East Muskerry'. *JCHAS* Vol. 52.
18. *Illustrated Guide to Irish Islands* 1905.
19. Jones F. *The Holy Wells of Wales*.
20. Lynch J. 'Antiquities around St. Finan's Bay, Co. Kerry'. *JRSAI* Vol. 32.
21. MacGill P.J. *Ardara* Nd.
22. MacNeil Maire. *The Festival of Lughnasa*. 1962.

23. MacParlan J. *Statistical Survey of the County Donegal*.
24. MacParlan J. *Statistical Survey of the County Leitrim*. 1802.
25. MacRitchie D. 'Note on Holed Stones'. *JRSAI* Vol. 22.
26. Morris H. 'The Holy Wells of Donegal'. *Bealoideas* 1956.
27. Murphy W. 'The Pattern of Mullinakill'. *Old Kilkenny Review* 1970.
28. O'Donnell M. *Betha Colaimb Cille*. Ed. Kelleher 1918.
29. O'Donovan et al. *Ordnance Survey Letters*.
30. O Dubhthaigh B. 'Tobar Aibheog'. *DA* 1968.
31. O Maidin P. 'Pococke's Tour of South and South West of Ireland'. *JCHAS* Vol. 65.
32. O'Reilly P.J. 'Tobernea Holy Well'. *JRSAI* Vol. 32.
33. O'Toole E. 'The Holy Wells of Co. Carlow'. *Bealoideas* 1933.
34. Page J.R. *Ireland: its evils traced to their source*. 1836.
35. Patterson T.G.F. 'The Cult of the Well in Co. Armagh'. *UJA* Vol. 11.
36. Piers H. 'Description of Westmeath'. *Collectaniae de Rebus Hibernicis L* 1786.
37. Pococke R. *A Tour of Ireland*. 1752.
38. Price L. 'Rock Basins or Bullauns'. *JRSAI* Vol. 89.
39. Purser O. 'St. John's Stone at Drumcullen Abbey'. *JRSAI* Vol. 48.
40. Rolleston T.W. 'The Church of St. Patrick on Caher Island'. *JRSAI* 1901.
41. Shaw-Mason. *Parochial Survey*. 3 Vols.
42. Smith C. *History of Kerry*. 1756.
43. Stokes M. 'St. Beoc of Wexford'. *JRSAI* Vol. 23.
44. Swire O.F. *Skye: The Island and its legends*. 2nd Edition 1973.
45. Talbot-Crosbie B. 'Tober-na-Molt'. *Kerry Archeological Magazine* 1911.
46. Thackeray W.M. *The Irish Sketch Book* 1842.
47. 'Townland Survey of Co. Louth'. *CLAJ*
48. Ua Maolain S. 'Tobar na n-Aingeal' *DA* 1949.
49. Wakeman W.F. 'Holy Wells in the North West of Ireland'. *JRSAI* Vol. 15.
50. Wakeman W.F. 'Inis Muiredach and its Antiquities'. *JRSAI* Vol. 17.
51. Wakeman W.F. 'The Antiquities of Devenish'. *JRSAI* Vol. 13.
52. White J. Grove. *Historical Notes on Buttevant* etc. 3 Vols.
53. Wilde W.R. 'Bleeding Cattle'. *JRSAI* Vol. 11 p. 248.
54. Wilde W.R. 'Glendalough Pattern'. *JRSAI* Vol. 12 p. 449.
55. Wilde W.R. *Loch Coirib*. 4th Edition 1955.
56. Wilde W.R. *The Boyne and Blackwater*. 3rd Edition 1949

Index

163

Index

Index

Index

Index